Be prepared...
To learn...
To succeed...

Get **REA**dy. It all starts here. REA's preparation for the Ohio Graduation Test is **fully aligned** with the Standards of the Ohio Department of Education.

Visit us online at
www.rea.com

About Research & Education Association

Founded in 1959, Research & Education Association is dedicated to publishing the finest and most effective educational materials—including software, study guides, and test preps—for students in middle school, high school, college, graduate school, and beyond. Today, REA's wide-ranging catalog is a leading resource for teachers, students, and professionals. We invite you to visit us at *www.rea.com* to find out how REA is making the world smarter.

Acknowledgments

We would like to thank REA's Larry B. Kling, Vice President, Editorial, for supervising development; Pam Weston, Vice President, Publishing, for setting the quality standards for production integrity and managing the publication to completion; Christine Reilley, Senior Editor, for project management and preflight editorial review; Diane Goldschmidt, Senior Editor, for post-production quality assurance; Michael Reynolds, Senior Editor, for coordinating revisions; Barbara McGowran for copyediting the manuscript; Terry Casey for indexing; Christine Saul, Senior Graphic Artist, for cover design; Jeff LoBalbo, Senior Graphic Artist, for post-production file mapping; and Rachel DiMatteo, Graphic Designer, for typesetting revisions.

We also gratefully acknowledge the writers, educators, and editors of REA and Northeast Editing for content development and Matrix Publishing for page design and typesetting.

Ready, Set, Go!™

OGT

Reading & Writing

Staff of Research & Education Association

 *Research & Education Association*

The standards presented in this book were created and implemented by the Ohio Department of Education (ODE). For further information, visit the ODE website at *www.ode.state.oh.us.*

Research & Education Association
61 Ethel Road West
Piscataway, New Jersey 08854
E-mail: info@rea.com

Ready, Set, Go!™
Ohio Graduation Test, Reading and Writing

Published 2009

Copyright © 2007 by Research & Education Association, Inc. All rights reserved. No part of this book may be reproduced in any form without permission of the publisher.

Printed in the United States of America

Library of Congress Control Number 2006930580

ISBN-13: 978-0-7386-0192-2
ISBN-10: 0-7386-0192-6

REA® is a registered trademark of Research & Education Association, Inc.

Contents

Section 1: Reading

Section 2: Writing

Passing the Ohio Graduation Test (OGT) in Reading and Writing

About This Book

This book will provide you with accurate and complete representation of the Ohio Graduation Test (OGT) in reading and the OGT in writing. Inside are reviews designed to give you the information and strategies you need to do well on these tests. Four practice tests are provided, two based on the official OGT in reading and two based on the official OGT in writing. The practice tests contain every type of question you can expect to encounter on the actual tests. Following each practice test is an answer key with detailed explanations to help you completely understand the test material.

About the Test

Who Takes These Tests, and What Are They Used For?

The OGT is given to all students throughout Ohio beginning in the spring of students' tenth-grade year. It is given to ensure that graduating students have mastered essential core academic content and skills. The test is given in five content areas: reading, writing, mathematics, science and social studies. Students who do not pass the OGT in the tenth grade will have four more opportunities to retake and pass the OGT before the end of their twelfth-grade year.

The OGT measures achievement in the skills and competencies outlined in Ohio's Academic Content Standards. The OGT in reading and OGT in writing measure achievement specifically according to the state's English Language Arts (ELA) Academic Content Standards. The OGT ensures that all graduating students demonstrate at least a tenth-grade proficiency in all five content areas. Students must pass each test to earn a high school diploma. A student who does not pass all five tests can still earn a diploma if he or she meets *all* the following requirements:

- Passed four of the five tests and missed passing the fifth test by no more than 10 points

- Has a 97 percent attendance rate (excluding excused absences) for all four years of high school and no expulsion in high school

- Has a grade point average of 2.5 out of 4.0 in the subject area missed and completed the curriculum requirement in the subject area missed

- Has participated in any intervention programs offered by the school and has a 97 percent attendance rate in any program offered outside the normal school day

- Obtains letters of recommendation from each teacher in the subject area not missed

Is There a Registration Fee?

No. Because all Ohio public and community or nonchartered high school students are required to take the OGT and pass the tests to receive a high school diploma, no fee is required.

When and Where Is the Test Given?

The OGT is first administered to Ohio high school students in the spring of their tenth-grade year. Makeup testing is offered a week after administration. Students will have several opportunities to take the OGT in each content area before the end of their twelfth-grade year. Tests are administered as follows:

- Spring of tenth grade

- Summer between tenth and eleventh grades (optional)

- Fall and spring of eleventh grade

- Summer between eleventh and twelfth grades (optional)

- Fall and spring of twelfth grade

Test Accommodations and Special Situations

Every student in Ohio must take the OGT or an alternative assessment. Every effort is made to provide a level playing field for students with disabilities taking the OGT and seeking a standard high school diploma. Accommodations are made for students who meet certain criteria, such as students with disabilities or limited English proficiency.

A student with significant cognitive disabilities and whose Individual Education Plan requires the student to take a different test can take the OGT Alternate Assessment for Students with Disabilities. This test measures achievement based on criteria that reflect the achievement of the individual student. For more information about accommodations and the OGT Alternate Assessment, go to the Ohio Department of Education website at *www.ode.state.oh.us*. Students can also ask questions of their school counselors.

Additional Information and Support

Additional resources to help you prepare to take the OGT can be found on the Ohio Department of Education website at *www.ode.state.oh.us*.

How to Use This Book

What Do I Study First?

Read over the review sections and the suggestions for test taking. Studying the review sections thoroughly will reinforce the basic skills you need to do well on the test. Be sure to take the practice tests to become familiar with the format and procedures involved with taking the actual OGT.

When Should I Start Studying?

It is never too early to start studying for the OGT. The earlier you begin, the more time you will have to sharpen your skills. Do not procrastinate! Cramming is *not* an effective way to study, because it does now allow you the time needed to learn the test material. The sooner you learn the format of the exam, the more time you will have to familiarize yourself with its content.

Format of the OGT

Overview of the OGT

The OGT in reading and writing are designed to test students' abilities to read and write, and also tests their knowledge of basic literary concepts and familiarity with basic writing strategies. The OGT in reading requires students to answer thirty-two multiple-choice questions, four short-response questions and two extended-response questions on the reading process, reading application and vocabulary. Passages on this test may be literary or informational.

The OGT in writing requires students to compose essays in response to two writing prompts and to answer ten multiple-choice questions and one short-response question on the writing process.

Scoring of the OGT

On the OGT in reading, each multiple-choice question is worth 1 point, each short-response question is worth 2 points, and each extended-response question is worth 4 points, for a total of 38 items and 48 possible points.

Student responses on the OGT in writing are assessed by two readers. Each reader assigns a score of 0 to 6 for writing applications and a score of 0 to 3 for writing conventions. The scores assigned by each reader are then added together. Because students are required to respond to two writing prompts, a total of 36 points may be achieved on the writing prompt portion of the OGT in writing. Additionally, each multiple-choice question is worth 1 point, and the short-response question is worth 2 points, for a total of 13 items and 48 possible points.

Test-Taking Strategies

What to Do Before the Test

- Pay attention in class.

- Carefully work through the review sections of this book. Mark any topics that you find difficult so you can focus on them while studying and get extra help if necessary.

- Take the practice tests and become familiar with the format of the OGT. When you are practicing, simulate the conditions under which you will be taking the actual test. Stay calm and pace yourself. After simulating the test only a couple of times, you will feel more confident, and this will boost your chances of doing well.

- You can relieve test anxiety, build confidence, and increase test success by being well prepared. A lot of test anxiety and stress will go away if you keep up with homework assignments and class work. Then, you can focus on the test with a clearer, more confident mind. It will help to talk to your parents and teachers if you are feeling nervous about this test or tests in general. They may be able to suggest some useful strategies to help you feel more relaxed so you can do your best on tests.

What to Do During the Test

- Read all the possible answers. Just because you think you have found the correct response, do not automatically assume that it is the best answer. Read through each answer choice to be sure that you are not making a mistake by jumping to conclusions.

- Use the process of elimination. Go through each answer to a question and eliminate as many of the answer choices as possible. By eliminating two answer choices, you will give yourself a better chance of getting the item correct, because you will have only two other choices to choose from.

- Work quickly and steadily, and avoid focusing on any one question for too long. Taking the practice tests in this book will help you learn to budget your time on the actual test.

- Work on the easiest questions first. If you find yourself working too long on one question, make a mark next to it on your test booklet and continue. After you have answered all the questions you know, go back to the ones you skipped.

- Be sure that the answer oval you are marking corresponds to the number of the question in the test booklet. Because the multiple-choice sections are graded by machine, marking one wrong answer can throw off your answer key and your score. Be extremely careful.

- Work from the answer choices. You can use a multiple-choice format to your advantage by working backward from the answer choices to answer the question. You may be able to make an educated guess after eliminating choices that you know do not fit the question.

Benchmarks of the OGT

Chapters	Benchmarks
Chapter 1: Vocabulary, Part 1	**Acquisition of Vocabulary** A. Use context clues and text structures to determine the meaning of new vocabulary. D. Explain how different events have influenced and changed the English language. E. Apply knowledge of roots and affixes to determine the meanings of complex words and subject-area vocabulary. **Grade Level Indicators** 1. Define unknown words through context clues and the author's use of comparison, contrast and cause and effect. 4. Examine and discuss ways historical events have influenced the English language. 5. Use knowledge of Greek, Latin and Anglo-Saxon roots, prefixes and suffixes to understand complex words and new subject-area vocabulary (e.g., unknown words in science, mathematics, social studies).

Chapter 2: Vocabulary, Part 2	**Acquisition of Vocabulary** C. Recognize the importance and function of figurative language. **Grade Level Indicators** 3. Infer the literal and figurative meanings of words and phrases and discuss the function of figurative language, including metaphors, similes, idioms and puns. **Reading Applications: Literary Text** F. Identify and analyze how an author uses figurative language, sound devices and literary techniques to shape plot, set meaning and develop tone. **Grade Level Indicators** 7. Recognize how irony is used in a literary text. 8. Analyze the author's use of point of view, mood and tone. 9. Explain how authors use symbols to create broader meanings. 10. Describe the effect of using sound devices in literary texts (e.g., to create rhythm, to appeal to the senses or to establish mood). 11. Explain ways in which an author develops a point of view and style (e.g., figurative language, sentence structure and tone), and cite specific examples from the text.
Chapter 3: Main Idea, Theme and Supporting Details	**Reading Process: Concepts of Print, Comprehension Strategies and Self-Monitoring Strategies** A. Apply reading comprehension strategies to understand grade-appropriate text. **Grade Level Indicators** 1. Apply reading comprehension strategies, including making predictions, comparing and contrasting, recalling and summarizing, and making inferences and drawing conclusions. **Reading Applications: Literary Text** E. Analyze the use of a genre to express a theme or topic. **Grade Level Indicators** 6. Analyze how an author's choice of genre affects the expression of a theme or topic.
Chapter 4: Evaluating Information	**Reading Process: Concepts of Print, Comprehension Strategies and Self-Monitoring Strategies** A. Apply reading comprehension strategies to understand grade-appropriate text. B. Demonstrate comprehension of print and electronic text by responding to questions (literal, inferential, evaluative and synthesizing). **Grade Level Indicators** 1. Apply reading comprehension strategies, including making predictions, comparing and contrasting, recalling and summarizing, and making inferences and drawing conclusions. 2. Answer literal, inferential, evaluative and synthesizing questions to demonstrate comprehension of grade-appropriate print texts and electronic and visual media.

Chapter 5: Author's Purpose	**Reading Applications: Informational, Technical and Persuasive Text** B. Identify examples of rhetorical devices and valid and invalid inferences, and explain how authors use these devices to achieve their purposes and reach their intended audiences. D. Explain and analyze how an author appeals to an audience and develops an argument or viewpoint in text. **Grade Level Indicators** 4. Assess the adequacy, accuracy and appropriateness of an author's details, identifying persuasive techniques (e.g., bandwagon, testimonial, transfer, glittering generalities, emotional word repetition, bait and switch) and examples of propaganda, bias and stereotyping. 5. Analyze an author's implicit and explicit argument, perspective or viewpoint in text. 6. Identify appeals to authority, reason and emotion. 8. Identify the features of rhetorical devices used in common types of public documents, including newspaper editorials and speeches.
Chapter 6: Literary Texts	**Reading Applications: Literary Text** A. Analyze interactions between characters in literary text and how the interactions affect the plot. C. Identify the structural elements of the plot and explain how an author develops conflicts and plot to pace the events in literary text. **Grade Level Indicators** 1. Compare and contrast an author's use of direct and indirect characterization, and ways in which characters reveal traits about themselves, including dialect, dramatic monologues and soliloquies. 3. Distinguish how conflicts, parallel plots and subplots affect the pacing of action in literary text. 7. Explain how literary techniques, including foreshadowing and flashback, are used to shape the plot of a literary text 8. Recognize how irony is used in a literary text.
Chapter 7: Nonfiction Texts	**Reading Applications: Informational, Technical and Persuasive Text** A. Evaluate how features and characteristics make information accessible and usable and how structures help authors achieve their purposes. C. Analyze whether graphics supplement textual information and promote the author's purpose. **Grade Level Indicators** 1. Identify and understand organizational patterns (e.g., cause-effect, problem-solution) and techniques, including repetition of ideas, syntax and word choice, that authors use to accomplish their purposes and reach their intended audiences. 3. Analyze information found in maps, charts, tables, graphs, diagrams, cutaways and overlays. 7. Compare and contrast the effectiveness of the features (e.g., format, sequence, headers) used in various consumer documents (e.g., warranties, product information, instructional materials), functional or workplace documents (e.g., job-related materials, memoranda, instructions) and public documents (e.g., speeches, newspaper editorials).

Chapter 8: Writing an Essay

Writing Applications

C. Produce letters (e.g., business letters, letters to the editor, job applications) that follow the conventional style appropriate to the text, include appropriate details and exclude extraneous details and inconsistencies.

E. Write a persuasive piece that states a clear position, includes relevant information and offers compelling evidence in the form of facts and details.

Grade Level Indicators

3. Write business letters, letters to the editor and job applications that do the following:
   a. Address audience needs, stated purpose and context in a clear and efficient manner
   b. Follow the conventional style appropriate to the text, using proper technical terms
   c. Include appropriate facts and details
   d. Exclude extraneous details and inconsistencies
   e. Provide a sense of closure to the writing

4. Write informational essays or reports, including research, that do the following:
   a. Pose relevant and tightly drawn questions that engage the reader
   b. Provide a clear and accurate perspective on the subject
   c. Create an organizing structure appropriate to the purpose, audience and context
   d. Support the main ideas with facts, details, examples and explanations from sources
   e. Document sources and include bibliographies

5. Write persuasive compositions that do the following:
   a. Support arguments with detailed evidence
   b. Exclude irrelevant information
   c. Cite sources of information

Writing Conventions

A. Use correct spelling conventions.
B. Use correct punctuation and capitalization.
C. Demonstrate understanding of the grammatical conventions of the English language.

Grade Level Indicators

1. Use correct spelling conventions.
2. Use correct capitalization and punctuation.
3. Use clauses (e.g., main, subordinate) and phrases (e.g., gerund, infinitive, participial).
4. Use parallel structure to present items in a series and items juxtaposed for emphasis.
5. Use proper placement of modifiers.

Chapter 9: Revising and Editing

Writing Processes

A. Formulate writing ideas and identify a topic appropriate to the purpose and audience.
B. Determine the usefulness of organizers and apply appropriate prewriting tasks.
C. Use revision strategies to improve the style, variety of sentence structure, clarity of the controlling idea, logic, effectiveness of word choice and transitions between paragraphs, passages or ideas.
D. Edit to improve sentence fluency, grammar and usage.
E. Apply tools to judge the quality of writing.

Grade Level Indicators

2. Determine the usefulness of and apply appropriate prewriting tasks (e.g., background reading, interviews or surveys).
3. Establish and develop a clear thesis statement for informational writing or a clear plan or outline for narrative writing.
4. Determine a purpose and audience and plan strategies (e.g., adapting focus, content structure and point of view) to address purpose and audience.
5. Use organizational strategies (e.g., notes, outlines) to plan writing.
6. Organize writing to create a coherent whole with an effective and engaging introduction, body and conclusion, and a closing sentence that summarizes, extends or elaborates on points or ideas in the writing.
7. Use a variety of sentence structures and lengths (e.g., simple, compound and complex sentences; parallel or repetitive sentence structure).
8. Use paragraph form in writing, including topic sentences that arrange paragraphs in a logical sequence, using effective transitions and closing sentences and maintaining coherence across the whole through the use of parallel structures.
9. Use language, including precise nouns, action verbs, sensory details and colorful modifiers, and style that are appropriate to audience and purpose, and use techniques to convey a personal style and voice.
11. Reread and analyze clarity of writing, consistency of point of view and effectiveness of organizational structure.
12. Add and delete information and details to better elaborate on stated central idea and more effectively accomplish purpose.
13. Rearrange words, sentences and paragraphs, and add transitional words and phrases to clarify meaning and maintain consistent style, tone and voice.
15. Proofread writing, edit to improve conventions (e.g., grammar, spelling, punctuation and capitalization), identify and correct fragments and run-ons, and eliminate inappropriate slang or informal language.

Section 1
Reading

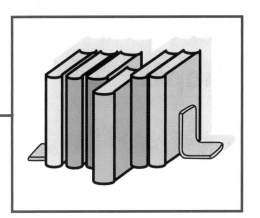

Chapter 1
Vocabulary, Part 1

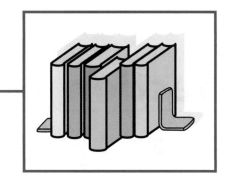

Benchmark

Acquisition of Vocabulary

A   Use context clues and text structures to determine the meaning of new vocabulary.

D   Explain how different events have influenced and changed the English language.

E   Apply knowledge of roots and affixes to determine the meanings of complex words and subject-area vocabulary.

Grade Level Indicators

1   Define unknown words through context clues and the author's use of comparison, contrast and cause and effect.

4   Examine and discuss ways historical events influenced the English language.

5   Use knowledge of Greek, Latin and Anglo-Saxon roots, prefixes and suffixes to understand complex words and new subject-area vocabulary (e.g., unknown words in science, mathematics, social studies).

Deriving Meaning

You acquire knowledge of vocabulary through the reading you do both inside and outside the classroom. On the OGT, you will be expected to use context clues and word structures to figure out the meanings of unfamiliar words or to apply new meanings to words you already know.

Context Clues

Vocabulary questions on the OGT typically will ask you to define a word used in a passage. You can often figure out a word's meaning by looking at the **context** of the word, meaning the words and sentences around it. Consider this example:

> Kirk was a huge hunk of a dog. When standing upright on his hind legs, he could easily rest his front paws on a man's shoulders. His enormous presence scared most passersby when Kirk strolled in the park on his daily walk on the leash. Other dogs, too, shunned Kirk, fearing death or severe injury should Kirk decide to clamp down on their flesh with his crushing jaws. No one had reason to worry, however. Terrified of squirrels and distrustful of robins and butterflies, Kirk was the most <u>docile</u> dog in the world.

> Use the context of this passage to determine the meaning of the word <u>docile</u>. Write the meaning of the word on the line below.

_____

Word Structure

Understanding the meaning of a word's parts can also help you determine its meaning. Many words contain some or all of these parts:

- Prefix

- Root

- Suffix

The **root** of a word is a word in its simplest form. The word *desire* is a root word. It does not have a prefix or suffix added to it; it is simply a root. *Desire* means *to want*. Letters added to the beginning of a word are called a **prefix**, and letters added to the end of a word are called a **suffix**. (See the charts in this section for some common prefixes and suffixes.) If you add the prefix *un-* and the suffix *-able* to *desire*, you create the word *undesirable*, which means *not desirable* or *not wanted*.

If you know the meaning of a word's prefix, root or suffix, you can often determine the meaning of the word. Consider this example:

> I go for a walk each day at lunch. Getting some exercise helps <u>rejuvenate</u> my mind and body.

What does the word <u>rejuvenate</u> mean?

    A. keep safe

    B. make fresh

    C. keep healthy

    D. relax

If you know that the prefix *re-* means *again*, it can help you figure out the meaning of *rejuvenate—to revive or make fresh*. Answer choice B is the best answer.

Make flashcards to help you study the word parts in each of the following tables. Knowing the meaning of these word parts will help you answer OGT vocabulary questions correctly.

Prefix	Meaning
anti-	against
anthro-	man
arch-	main
auto-	self
bi-	two
bio-	life
circum-	around
de-	the opposite of
dis-	not, the opposite of, completely
im-	not
mal-	bad
mis-	badly or wrongly; not
pre-	before
pro-	for; in favor of
sub-	below

super-	above; better
tele-	far; away
trans-	across
un-	not
uni-	one
via-	by way of

Suffix	Meaning
-able	able to
-er	doer
-ful	full of
-logy	the study of
-ly	like
-ment	state
-ness	state of being
-ous	full of

Passage 1

Read the following passage. Then answer the questions that follow. Use the Tip below each question to help you choose the correct answer. When you finish, read the answer explanations at the end of this chapter.

Departure (Excerpt from *Winesburg, Ohio*)
by Sherwood Anderson

1   Young George Willard got out of bed at four in the morning. It was April and the young tree leaves were just coming out of their buds. The trees along the residence streets in Winesburg are maple and the seeds are winged. When the wind blows they whirl crazily about, filling the air and making a carpet underfoot.

2   George came downstairs into the hotel office carrying a brown leather bag. His trunk was packed for <u>departure</u>. Since two o'clock he had been awake thinking of the journey he was about to take and wondering what he would find at the end of his journey. The boy who slept in the hotel office lay on a cot by the door. His mouth was open and he snored lustily. George crept past the cot and went out into the silent deserted main street. The east was pink with the dawn and long streaks of light climbed into the sky where a few stars still shone.

3   Beyond the last house on Trunion Pike in Winesburg there is a great stretch of open fields. The fields are owned by farmers who live in town and drive homeward at evening along Trunion Pike in light creaking wagons. In the fields are planted berries and small fruits. In the late afternoon in the hot summers when the road and the fields are covered with dust, a smoky haze lies over the great flat basin of land. To look across it is like looking out across the sea. In the spring when the land is green the effect is somewhat different. The land becomes a wide green billiard table on which tiny human insects toil up and down.

4   All through his boyhood and young manhood George Willard had been in the habit of walking on Trunion Pike. He had been in the midst of the great open place on winter nights when it was covered with snow and only the moon looked down at him; he had been there in the fall when bleak winds blew and on summer evenings when the air vibrated with the song of insects. On the April morning he wanted to go there again, to walk again in the silence. He did walk to where the road dipped down by a little stream two miles from town and then turned and walked silently back again. When he got to Main Street clerks were sweeping the sidewalks before the stores. "Hey you, George. How does it feel to be going away?" they asked.

5   The westbound train leaves Winesburg at seven forty-five in the morning. Tom Little is conductor. His train runs from Cleveland to where it connects with a great trunk line railroad with terminals in Chicago and New York. Tom has what in railroad circles is called an "easy run." Every evening he returns to his family. In the fall and spring he spends his Sundays fishing in Lake Erie. He has a round red face and small blue eyes. He knows the people in the towns along his railroad better than a city man knows the people who live in his apartment building.

6   George came down the little incline from the New Willard House at seven o'clock. Tom Willard carried his bag. The son had become taller than the father.

7   On the station platform everyone shook the young man's hand. More than a dozen people waited about. Then they talked of their own affairs. Even Will Henderson, who was lazy and often slept until nine, had got out of bed. George was embarrassed. Gertrude Wilmot, a tall thin woman of fifty who worked in the Winesburg post office, came along the station platform. She had never before paid any attention to George. Now she stopped and put out her hand. In two words she voiced what everyone felt. "Good luck," she said sharply and then turning went on her way.

8   When the train came into the station George felt relieved. He scampered hurriedly aboard. Helen White came running along Main Street hoping to have a parting word with him, but he had found a seat and did not see her. When the train started Tom Little punched his ticket, grinned and, although he knew George well and knew on what adventure he was just setting out, made no comment. Tom had seen a thousand George Willards go out of their towns to the city. It was a commonplace enough incident with him. In the smoking car there was a man who had just invited Tom to go on a fishing trip to Sandusky Bay. He wanted to accept the invitation and talk over details.

9   George glanced up and down the car to be sure no one was looking, then took out his pocket-book and counted his money. His mind was occupied with a desire not to appear green. Almost the last words his father had said to him concerned the matter of his behavior when he got to the city. "Be a sharp one," Tom Willard had said. "Keep your eyes on your money. Be awake. That's the ticket. Don't let anyone think you're a greenhorn."

10   After George counted his money he looked out of the window and was surprised to see that the train was still in Winesburg.

11   The young man, going out of his town to meet the adventure of life, began to think but he did not think of anything very big or dramatic. Things like his mother's death, his departure from Winesburg, the uncertainty of his future life in the city, the serious and larger aspects of his life did not come into his mind.

12   He thought of little things—Turk Smollet wheeling boards through the main street of his town in the morning, a tall woman, beautifully gowned, who had once stayed overnight at his father's hotel, Butch Wheeler the lamp lighter of Winesburg hurrying through the streets on a summer evening and holding a torch in his hand, Helen White standing by a window in the Winesburg post office and putting a stamp on an envelope.

13   The young man's mind was carried away by his growing passion for dreams. One looking at him would not have thought him particularly sharp. With the recollection of little things occupying his mind he closed his eyes and leaned back in the car seat. He stayed that way for a long time and when he aroused himself and again looked out of the car window the town of Winesburg had disappeared and his life there had become but a background on which to paint the dreams of his manhood.

? Questions

1 "His trunk was packed for <u>departure</u>." (paragraph 2)

In this excerpt from the passage, the word <u>departure</u> means

A. the time being.

B. the act of vacationing.

C. the last time.

D. the act of leaving.

 TIP If you are not sure of the meaning of the word, re-read the sentences that surround it. Look for clues that might help you figure out the meaning.

2 In paragraph 9, the speaker explains that George's "mind was occupied with a desire not to appear <u>green</u>."

Which definition represents the intended meaning of the word <u>green</u>?

A. jealous

B. sick

C. inexperienced

D. wealthy

 TIP Reread the sentence and the sentences that surround it. Try to figure out why the speaker would describe George's feelings in this way.

3 "'Be a <u>sharp</u> one,' Tom Willard had said."

In this excerpt from paragraph 9, the word <u>sharp</u> means

A. distinct.

B. able to cut.

C. harsh.

D. intelligent.

 TIP Carefully read all of the answer choices before deciding which one best reflects how the author uses the word in the passage.

Passage 2

Read the following poem. Then answer the questions that follow. Use the Tip below each question to help you choose the correct answer. When you finish, read the answer explanations at the end of this chapter.

Annabel Lee
by Edgar Allan Poe

1   It was many and many a year ago,

In a kingdom by the sea,

That a maiden there lived whom you may know

By the name of Annabel Lee;

And this maiden she lived with no other thought

Than to love and be loved by me.

2   *She* was a child and *I* was a child,

In this kingdom by the sea:

But we loved with a love that was more than love—

I and my Annabel Lee;

With a love that the wingéd seraphs of Heaven

<u>Coveted</u> her and me.

3   And this was the reason that, long ago,

In this kingdom by the sea,

A wind blew out of a cloud by night

Chilling my Annabel Lee;

So that her highborn kinsmen came

And <u>bore</u> her away from me,

To shut her up in a sepulchre

In this kingdom by the sea.

4   The angels, not half so happy in Heaven,

Went envying her and me:—

Yes! that was the reason (as all men know,

In this kingdom by the sea)

That the wind came out of the cloud, chilling

And killing my Annabel Lee.

5 But our love it was stronger by far than the love

Of those who were older than we—

Of many far wiser than we—

And neither the angels in heaven above,

Nor the demons down under the sea,

Can ever <u>dissever</u> my soul from the soul

Of the beautiful Annabel Lee:—

6 For the moon never beams without bringing me dreams

Of the beautiful Annabel Lee;

And the stars never rise but I see the bright eyes

Of the beautiful Annabel Lee;

And so, all the night-tide, I lie down by the side

Of my darling, my darling, my life and my bride,

In her sepulchre there by the sea—

In her tomb by the side of the sea.

? Questions

4   As used in stanza 2, <u>coveted</u> means something or someone that is

   A. noticed.

   B. adopted.

   C. desired.

   D. injured.

 Try inserting each definition to see which fits best, and look for clues from the poem to help you to better understand the word's meaning.

5   As used in stanza 3, <u>bore</u> means the same as which phrase?

   A. equipped with

   B. took possession of

   C. carried away with difficulty

   D. exerted influence over

 Reread the stanza and think about what Annabel Lee's kinsmen did to her. Then choose the answer that fits best.

6   "And neither the angels in heaven above,
   Nor the demons down under the sea,
   Can ever <u>dissever</u> my soul from the soul
   Of the beautiful Annabel Lee." (stanza 5)

   In this excerpt from the poem, <u>dissever</u> means

   A. sentence.

   B. respect.

   C. separate.

   D. remarry.

 Think about the author's message in this poem. Look at the prefix and root word. Then read the answer choices. Which is correct?

Passage 3

Read the following passage. Then answer the questions that follow. Use the Tip below each question to help you choose the correct answer. When you finish, read the answer explanations at the end of this chapter.

The Six Nations of the Iroquois

1   Long before the United States of America was created, a group of American Indians known as the Iroquois formed a united government of their own. Their government was known as the Six Nations of the Iroquois. It was so fair and effective that it helped to inspire the creation of the United States in 1776.

2   The history of the Iroquois reaches back thousands of years. Since ancient times, many American Indian tribes lived in the lands around New York State. Among these groups were the Mohawk, Seneca, Onondaga, Oneida and Cayuga. These five groups had been at odds with one another for many years. A mysterious man arrived in their lands with a plan for peace. Representatives of the five tribes met and listened to the words of their <u>eloquent</u> visitor. After that, they decided to make peace and unite into a single government. (Later, a sixth tribe, the Tuscarora, joined the group.)

3   The Six Nations government immediately proved its worth. The six tribes no longer had to waste time and energy fighting with one another. Instead, they could advance their cultures and defend themselves against common enemies. Among them, the members of the Six Nations controlled much of the land of the northeast. They referred to their shared lands as their Longhouse. They stationed powerful tribes to guard each end of it. By the 1600s, the Six Nations was a force to be reckoned with.

4   Colonists from Britain and France began gathering in North America. The Iroquois were pressed into making treaties and agreements with them. Although strictly honest in their dealings, the Iroquois understandably felt no deep loyalty to either side. Both sides were frequently unfair and often brutal to the American Indians and took much of their lands. The

Iroquois created a kind of survival technique that involved playing the British and French against one another. By keeping the Europeans angry with one another, the Iroquois could gain benefits and keep more of their power.

5   However, the Iroquois could not maintain their "catbird seat" between the European competitors for long. As the British and French began to fight one another, the Iroquois were drawn in and forced to choose sides. Later, during the Revolutionary War, they were again forced to choose. That time, they had to decide whether to join the British or the Americans. The Six Nations became desegregated during those wars. By around 1800, the power of the Iroquois had been broken.

6   Although the Americans, the newcomers to the continent, claimed control over the land, the Iroquois people never died out. Today Iroquois groups that supported the Americans in the Revolution still exist, and their members are U.S. citizens. Most live on reservations in New York State, Oklahoma and Wisconsin. Many thousands of other Iroquois people now live in Canada. These people are the <u>descendants</u> of the Iroquois who supported the British.

7   The original lands once owned by the Iroquois are now used by non-Indian citizens. These lands have been changed greatly from their natural state. Today they are largely covered in highways, railroads, reservoirs, power lines and other technologies. Ironically, most modern Iroquois reservations have not been given the benefits of such helpful projects. Because of this, the standard of living on Iroquois reservations is usually lower than the communities around them.

8   Nevertheless, Iroquois reservations are not crude or primitive places. Like most communities, they respect the symbols and customs of their ancestors, but they have not been "left behind" in the past. Most reservations today are fully <u>modernized</u>. Some visitors expect to see ancient shelters like teepees and wigwams still in use. These visitors are surprised to realize that most modern Iroquois live in frame or manufactured housing.

9   Many reservations are full of small businesses. These include markets, mills, repair shops and gas stations. The communities also support banks, libraries, sports arenas, museums, cultural centers and places of worship. Gaming is a major industry among some Indian groups. Tourists from all over the United States visit reservations to try their luck at casinos and bingo halls.

10   The other major industry, one that provides a link between modern Iroquois and their ancient ancestry, is art. The crafts of the Iroquois are unique and of increasing interest as the world becomes more reliant on <u>bland</u> manufactured items. Craftspeople among the American Indians carry on long, proud traditions and skills. They are masters of beadwork, basket and doll making and pottery.

11   Tourists purchase much of this art, which helps the economy of the reservations. It also enables Iroquois artists to spread their talents to other communities. Iroquois artwork is featured in many museums and at cultural festivals. Other forms of art, including music, dancing and storytelling, are also popular among modern Indians.

12   Despite the great changes and sufferings among the Iroquois, the Six Nations is still very much alive. Today Iroquois communities still select chiefs to represent them at the ongoing meetings of the Iroquois Counsel. The Six Nations government considers itself independent and free from the control of the U.S. or Canadian governments. The leaders and citizens of the Six Nations continue to work hard to benefit their people and preserve their customs into the future.

(?) Questions

7   "Representatives of the five tribes met and listened to the words of their <u>eloquent</u> visitor." (paragraph 2)

In this excerpt from the passage, the word eloquent means

A. expressive.

B. traditional.

C. perplexing.

D. threatening.

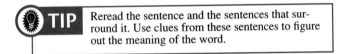
TIP   Reread the sentence and the sentences that surround it. Use clues from these sentences to figure out the meaning of the word.

8   According to the information given in paragraph 6, the word <u>descendants</u>, whose root is *descend*, must refer to

A. the people who worked to keep the Iroquois off reservations.

B. the people who go to the reservations to play at the casinos.

C. the people who now live on the reservations of the Iroquois.

D. the people who have proceeded from an ancestor or source.

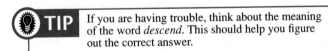
TIP   If you are having trouble, think about the meaning of the word *descend*. This should help you figure out the correct answer.

9   "Most reservations today are fully <u>modernized</u>." (paragraph 8)

Which phrase represents the meaning of <u>modernized</u>?

   A. simplified to make clearer

   B. used for practical purposes

   C. adapted for a particular use

   D. updated to current standards

 Consider the word as it is used in context. You might also want to consider the meaning of the root word, *modern*. This will help you discover the correct answer.

10 In paragraph 10, manufactured items are described as being "<u>bland</u>."

Which definition represents the intended meaning of the word bland?

   A. very affordable

   B. not distinctive

   C. liked by many people

   D. lacking taste

 Carefully read each answer choice before deciding which definition best fits the word as it is used in the passage. Look at how the word is used in the context of the sentence if you need more help.

Passage 4

Read the following passage. Then answer the questions that follow. Use the Tip below each question to help you choose the correct answer. When you finish, read the answer explanations at the end of this chapter.

Curious Crop Circles

1   Imagine for a moment that you are a farmer. One morning you awaken to find a large circular pattern in the middle of your fields. Where rows of wheat, soy or corn stood tall just yesterday, there is now a perfectly shaped circle. For many farmers around the world, this is a baffling reality. This strange <u>phenomenon</u> is known as a crop circle, and it is characterized by the symmetrical flattening of crops into a geometric pattern, usually occurring overnight when there are no witnesses. The formations generally appear between late spring and early autumn, with most circles discovered during the summer months. The United Kingdom has had the largest number of crop circles over the years, but countries like the United States, Germany, Canada and the Netherlands have reported an increase in incidents since the late twentieth century.

2   Crop circles first garnered international attention in the media during the early 1980s, when a series of circles was discovered in southern England. However, many argue that crop circles have been reported since the early seventeenth century. A tale dating back to 1678 tells of a farmer who refused to pay a laborer for mowing a field. That night, the field appeared to be on fire. When the farmer went to inspect his crops the following morning, instead of finding charred remains, he discovered that the field had actually been mowed, but by whom or

what he could not say. Although many dispute the validity of this early incident, others note that farmers have been reporting crop circles for generations.

3   Of course, the real mystery is who or what is behind the creation of these circles in the middle of the night. Theories explaining the existence of crop circles range from the mundane to the supernatural. Many feel that most crop circles are nothing but elaborate hoaxes <u>perpetrated</u> by people with nothing better to do with their time or looking for their fifteen minutes of fame.

4   Two of the most famous hoaxers were discovered in England. In 1991, Doug Bower and Dave Chorley claimed they had been staging crop circles for nearly fifteen years, creating more than 200 circles. The men said they would sneak into fields at night and use a wooden plank tied to some string to flatten the crops into circles while the owners of the fields were asleep. Even if Bower and Chorley were telling the truth, their story does not account for the more than 2,000 other circles reported around the country during the time they were working.

5   Today the debate over hoaxing continues. Professional circle makers have appeared on numerous television programs, trying to prove that crop circles, even the extremely complex ones, are made by people. Circle makers have created formations for everything from music videos to movies, like the 2002 film *Signs*. Several businesses use computer technology to create circle advertisements in fields where airplane passengers are most likely to spot them.

6   Still, crop circle researchers note several key differences between artificial and what they call authentic crop circles. First, researchers note that when an artificial pattern is formed, evidence of a human presence usually is left behind, like footprints in the soil or impressions from the tools that were used. Second, when a genuine formation is found, there are sometimes unexplainable changes to the environment that do not occur when a circle is the work of tricksters.

7   One especially interesting fact researchers point out is that particularly unyielding crops, like canola plants, tend to snap when they are bent by the tools many hoaxers use, whereas these same crops inexplicably bend in "legitimate" formations. Other important differences that researchers have noted between what they consider real crop circles and hoaxes are cellular changes in plants, changes in seeds and dehydrated soil in genuine cases.

8   The most popular, and the most controversial, theory of the cause of crop circles is that they are the work of extraterrestrial life forms trying to make contact with human beings. Proponents of this idea believe that the formations must be created by an intelligent life form and that the circles are far too intricate for even a small team of humans to create overnight without being caught. To support this claim, many people point to other strange phenomena that sometimes accompany crop circles as evidence of an alien presence. These reports include seeing balls of light and hearing unusual sounds in the areas where the circles are later discovered. Some believe that this theory might also explain the curious effect that some circles have on plants, but so far there is not enough conclusive evidence to <u>link</u> crop circles to an otherworldly force.

9   The search for a more terrestrial answer to the cause of crop circles continues. Some scientists believe that the earth itself is the cause of these mysterious events. One argument is that a shift in the earth's electromagnetic field would be enough to flatten crops without breaking them. Another idea is that changes in the weather patterns over the last few centuries could be the source of crop circles. Several other theories conclude that crop circles are probably more natural than <u>supernatural</u>.

10   Although some crop circles have proved to be nothing more than pranks, others are not so easy to dismiss. Until there is a clear-cut explanation for the phenomenon, it is likely that these mysterious formations will continue to fascinate researchers and other people worldwide for some time to come.

? Questions

11   "This strange <u>phenomenon</u> is known as a crop circle, and it is characterized by the symmetrical flattening of crops into a geometric pattern." (paragraph 1)

In this excerpt from paragraph 1, the word <u>phenomenon</u> means

   A. occurrence.

   B. experiment.

   C. celebration.

   D. distribution.

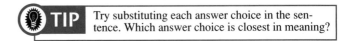 **TIP** Try substituting each answer choice in the sentence. Which answer choice is closest in meaning?

12   "Many feel that most crop circles are nothing but elaborate hoaxes <u>perpetrated</u> by people with nothing better to do with their time or looking for their fifteen minutes of fame." (paragraph 3)

Which phrase is closest in meaning to the word <u>perpetrated</u>?

   A. accepted

   B. attracted

   C. released

   D. performed

 TIP Try substituting each answer choice in the sentence with the word perpetrated. Which answer choice is closest in meaning?

13 "Some believe that this theory might also explain the curious effect that some circles have on plants, but so far there is not enough conclusive evidence to <u>link</u> crop circles to an otherworldly force." (paragraph 8)

In this excerpt from paragraph 8, the word <u>link</u> means

A. connect.

B. divide.

C. ring.

D. transmit.

 Read the sentence and try substituting each of the answer choices for the word *link*. Which makes the most sense?

14 "Several other theories conclude that crop circles are probably more natural than <u>supernatural</u>." (paragraph 9)

In this excerpt from the paragraph 9, <u>supernatural</u> means

A. strange.

B. likable.

C. difficult.

D. evident.

 Think about the information discussed in this passage. Then look at the prefix and root of the word *supernatural*. This should help you choose the best answer.

✔ Answers and Explanations

1 D

It is clear that Tom is going somewhere, because his trunk is packed. We cannot assume that he is going on vacation.

2 C

In this passage, the word *green* is used to reflect George's inexperience. The author explains that George does not want to appear unsure of what to do. When his father warns him to "be awake" and keep his eyes on his money, he is telling him to act as if he is an experienced traveler. Although the word *green* can also describe someone who looks sick, feels jealous or is wealthy, none of these descriptions fits George in this passage.

3 D

Here *sharp* means *intelligent*. Tom thinks that George will be all right as long as he makes smart decisions and is aware of his surroundings. The other answer choices do not fit within the context of the passage.

4 C

The word *coveted* means that the angels *desired* the love that the narrator shared with Annabel Lee. Because they could not have what they desired, Annabel Lee was taken from the narrator.

5 C

As used in the poem, the word *bore* means *carried away with difficulty*. This definition best fits the meaning of the word as the author uses it in the poem.

6 C

The prefix of the word *dissever* is *dis-*, which in this case means *completely*. The root of *dissever* is *sever*, which means *to separate*. The speaker is explaining that though Annabel Lee has physically been taken from him, there is no force in the world that can completely separate their souls.

7 A

The word *eloquent* means *expressive*. The other answer choices do not apply to the word as it is used in the passage.

8 D

The root word *descend* means *to come from* or *to be passed down from a source*. Therefore, the word *descendants* refers to the people that have proceeded from ancestors.

9 D

The word *modernized* means that the reservations are up-to-date and not stuck in the past the way people might think.

10 B

By looking at the sentence that contains the word *bland*, you can see that the author is using it to contrast the handmade items of the Iroquois with the manufactured items most of us buy in stores. Whereas the Iroquois' work has character, the manufactured items are not distinctive or lack character.

11 A

A *phenomenon* is any occurrence that can be perceived by the senses. The other definitions do not define this word correctly.

12 D

Someone who has *perpetrated* something is a person who is responsible for a certain action, right or wrong.

13 A

As it is used in the passage, the word *link* refers to a connection between crop circles and the existence of an otherworldly force.

14 A

The prefix of the word *supernatural* is *super-*, meaning *above* or *better*. The root of the word is *nature*. If something is "above nature," it is strange, or not natural.

Chapter 2

Vocabulary, Part 2

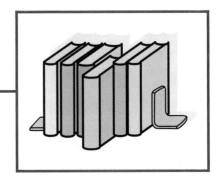

Benchmarks

Acquisition of Vocabulary

C. Recognize the importance and function of figurative language.

Grade Level Indicators

3. Infer the literal and figurative meanings of words and phrases and discuss the function of figurative language, including metaphors, similes, idioms and puns.

Reading Applications: Literary Text

F. Identify and analyze how an author uses figurative language, sound devices and literary techniques to shape plot, set meaning and develop tone.

Grade Level Indicators

7. Recognize how irony is used in a literary text.

8. Analyze the author's use of point of view, mood and tone.

9. Explain how authors use symbols to create broader meanings.

10. Describe the effect of using sound devices in literary texts (e.g., to create rhythm, to appeal to the senses or to establish mood).

11. Explain ways in which an author develops a point of view and style (e.g., figurative language, sentence structure and tone), and cite specific examples from the text.

Author's Word Choice

In Chapter 1, you learned how to identify the meanings of unfamiliar vocabulary words by using context clues and word roots. However, other questions on the OGT will test your understanding of vocabulary in a different way. These questions will ask you to analyze why authors use specific words or phrases in a selection. Throughout this book, you will see this type of question applied to the various genres of writing.

When an author writes, he or she must make hundreds of decisions about words, phrases and sentences for both **rhetorical** (relating to the creation of effective writing or speech) and **aesthetic** (relating to a beautiful appearance) reasons. Simply put, writers want their work to sound and look good to readers.

Choosing the right language to use in the right situation to achieve maximum effectiveness is called **diction**. Read these examples:

1. "Good afternoon. How are you doing today, Grandma?" asked Rose.

2. "Yo, Gram, what's up?" hollered Rose.

Essentially, these two sentences say the same thing. However, the diction the author chooses to use will determine whether readers perceive Rose as respectful (example 1) or disrespectful (example 2) to her grandmother.

Choosing how to put words together to make effective clauses and sentences is called **syntax**. When an author writes, he or she chooses words carefully to convey a specific message to readers. An author tries to use words that accurately describe tastes, sounds, sights, smells or feelings. By using words that appeal to readers' senses, an author can create vivid images in the minds of readers. Each time an author makes a deliberate word choice, it is meant not only to support the theme of the work but also to communicate his or her point of view or purpose for writing.

On the OGT, you might be asked to explain the effect of certain language choices. Some of the questions on the OGT will ask you to determine the meaning of figurative language and literary devices such as similes, metaphors, symbols and personification. Others might ask you to explain the meaning of idioms. For example, "You're in hot water" is an idiom meaning "You are in trouble." It does not literally mean that you are standing in hot water. Other questions might ask you to identify irony within a passage.

Tone and Mood

Some questions on the OGT will ask you about the tone or the mood of the story. The **tone** reflects the author's attitude about the subject of his or her writing. If an author is writing about a happy childhood memory, the tone might be whimsical or sentimental. If an author is writing a first-person story about a character who is upset, the tone might be angry or sarcastic. The mood of a piece of writing is the feeling the writing evokes in the reader. The **mood** might be cheerful, mysterious or sentimental. The following table gives some common words that are used to describe tone and mood.

Common Words Used to Describe Tone and Mood

ambivalent	encouraging	inspirational	remorseful
amused	enthusiastic	ironic	rude
angry	envious	judgmental	sad
anxious	excited	lighthearted	sarcastic
appreciative	fearful	malicious	sentimental
bewildered	formal	mischievous	serious
bitter	friendly	mysterious	sincere
bored	frustrated	nervous	snobbish
calm	gentle	neutral	suspenseful
cheerful	gloomy	nostalgic	sympathetic
concerned	honest	objective	tense
critical	hopeful	pensive	thankful
curious	humorous	pessimistic	tolerant
defensive	imaginative	proud	tragic
depressed	impersonal	reflective	vindictive
determined	indifferent	relaxed	whimsical
dissatisfied	innocent	relieved	worrisome

Passage 1

Read the following passage. Then answer the questions that follow. Use the Tip below each question to help you choose the correct answer. When you finish, read the answer explanations at the end of this chapter.

The Man He Killed
by Thomas Hardy

1   Had he and I but met

By some old ancient inn,

We should have sat us down to wet

Right many a nipperkin[1]!

2   "But ranged as infantry,

And staring face to face.

I shot at him and he at me,

And killed him in his place.

3   "I shot him dead because—

Because he was my foe,

Just so; my foe of course he was;

That's clear enough; although

4   "He thought he'd 'list perhaps,

Off-hand, like—just as I—

Was out of work—had sold his traps[2]—

No other reason why.

5   "Yes, quaint and curious war is!

You shoot a fellow down

You'd treat if met where any bar is,

Or help to half-a-crown.

—1902

1. *Nipperkin* = cup

2. *Traps* = his personal things

❓ Questions

1   What does the narrator mean when he says about the man he killed, "He thought he'd 'list perhaps, / Off-hand, like"? (stanza 4)

    A. The man joined the military because he had no other options.

    B. The man had just left his job as a professional salesman.

    C. The man did not give much thought to joining the military.

    D. The man did not think that he would ever have to fight in a war.

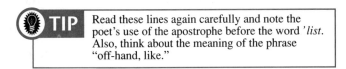

TIP: Read these lines again carefully and note the poet's use of the apostrophe before the word '*list*. Also, think about the meaning of the phrase "off-hand, like."

2   What is the intended effect of the narrator's description of war as "quaint and curious"? (stanza 5)

    A. It stresses the danger and uncertainty the narrator faced in the war.

    B. It expresses the narrator's sarcasm and criticism of the war.

    C. It demonstrates the narrator's fear of fighting in another war.

    D. It shows that the narrator has remorse over the destruction the war caused.

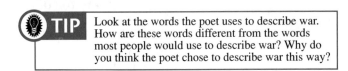

TIP: Look at the words the poet uses to describe war. How are these words different from the words most people would use to describe war? Why do you think the poet chose to describe war this way?

3   Identify two examples of how repetition is used in the poem. Write your answer in the space provided.

_____

TIP: Repetition occurs when a writer uses a word, phrase or situation more than once within a text to emphasize his or her point. Read the poem again, and look for examples of repetition. Why do you think the poet chose to use repetition in this poem?

Passage 2

Read the following passage. Then answer the questions that follow. Use the Tip below each question to help you choose the correct answer. When you finish, read the answer explanations at the end of this chapter.

Excerpt from *Up from Slavery: An Autobiography*
by Booker T. Washington

1   I was born a slave on a plantation in Franklin County, Virginia. I am not quite sure of the exact place or exact date of my birth, but at any rate I suspect I must have been born somewhere and at some time. As nearly as I have been able to learn, I was born near a cross-roads post-office called Hale's Ford, and the year was 1858 or 1859. I do not know the month or the day. The earliest impressions I can now recall are of the plantation and the slave quarters—the latter being the part of the plantation where the slaves had their cabins.

2   My life had its beginning in the midst of the most miserable, desolate, and discouraging surroundings. This was so, however, not because my owners were especially cruel, for they were not, as compared with many others. I was born in a typical log cabin, about fourteen by sixteen feet square. In this cabin I lived with my mother and a brother and sister till after the Civil War, when we were all declared free. . . .

3   The cabin was not only our living-place, but was also used as the kitchen for the plantation. My mother was the plantation cook. The cabin was without glass windows; it had only openings in the side which let in the light, and also the cold, chilly air of winter. There was a door to the cabin—that is, something that was called a door—but the uncertain hinges by which it was hung, and the large cracks in it, to say nothing of the fact that it was too small, made the room a very uncomfortable one. . . . There was no wooden floor in our cabin, the naked earth being used as a floor. In the centre of the earthen floor there was a large, deep opening covered with boards, which was used as a place in which to store sweet potatoes during the winter. An impression of this potato-hole is very distinctly engraved upon my memory, because I recall that during the process of putting the potatoes in or taking them out I would often come into possession of one or two, which I roasted and thoroughly enjoyed. There was no cooking-stove on our plantation, and all the cooking for the whites and slaves my mother had to do over an open fireplace, mostly in pots and "skillets." While the poorly built cabin caused us to suffer with cold in the winter, the heat from the open fireplace in summer was equally trying.

4   The early years of my life, which were spent in the little cabin, were not very different from those of thousands of other slaves. My mother, of course, had little time in which to give attention to the training of her children during the day. She snatched a few moments for our care in the early morning before her work began, and at night after the day's work was

done. One of my earliest recollections is that of my mother cooking a chicken late at night, and awakening her children for the purpose of feeding them. How or where she got it I do not know. I presume, however, it was procured from our owner's farm. Some people may call this theft. If such a thing were to happen now, I should condemn it as theft myself. But taking place at the time it did, and for the reason that it did, no one could ever make me believe that my mother was guilty of thieving. She was simply a victim of the system of slavery. I cannot remember having slept in a bed until after our family was declared free by the Emancipation Proclamation. Three children—John, my older brother, Amanda, my sister, and myself—had a pallet on the dirt floor, or, to be more correct, we slept in and on a bundle of filthy rags laid upon the dirt floor. . . .

5   I had no schooling whatever while I was a slave, though I remember on several occasions I went as far as the schoolhouse door with one of my young mistresses to carry her books. The picture of several dozen boys and girls in a schoolroom engaged in study made a deep impression upon me, and I had the feeling that to get into a schoolhouse and study in this way would be about the same as getting into paradise.

6   So far as I can now recall, the first knowledge that I got of the fact that we were slaves, and that freedom of the slaves was being discussed, was early one morning before day, when I was awakened by my mother kneeling over her children and fervently praying that Lincoln and his armies might be successful, and that one day she and her children might be free.

? Questions

4   Explain what the narrator means by the phrase "a victim of the system of slavery" (paragraph 4). Support your explanation by providing an example or piece of information from the passage.

 TIP Read the paragraph surrounding the phrase. What point is the writer trying to make with this statement?

5   What is the intended effect of the description in paragraph 5, that the narrator's visit to the school "made a deep impression upon" him?

A.   He was fascinated by the experience.

B.   He was annoyed by the experience.

C.   He was terrified by the experience.

D.   He was confused by the experience.

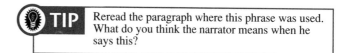

TIP   Reread the paragraph where this phrase was used. What do you think the narrator means when he says this?

6   Which sentence describes the intended effect of the statement "I am not quite sure of the exact place or exact date of my birth, but at any rate I suspect I must have been born somewhere and at some time"? (paragraph 1)

A.   It explains that it is not necessary to know where and when you were born.

B.   It demonstrates that the narrator has trouble remembering the past.

C.   It reinforces the idea that slaves were treated as property and not people.

D.   It shows that people in the past did not keep track of their birthdays.

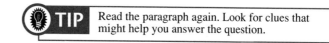

TIP   Read the paragraph again. Look for clues that might help you answer the question.

Passage 3

Read the following passage. Then answer the questions that follow. Use the Tip below each question to help you choose the correct answer. When you finish, read the answer explanations at the end of this chapter.

William Shakespeare: Poet and Playwright

1   From the finest universities to countless bedside tables and even the pages of the Internet, the words of William Shakespeare can be found in all four corners of the world. Shakespeare is arguably the most famous and one of the most well respected writers in the history of the English language. The writer's plays and poems have been translated into every current living language. Centuries after his death, Shakespeare's works are still examined by scholars, his words recited by lovers and his life and times explored by historians. However, despite being one of the most widely recognized figures in modern history, very little is known about the mysterious writer.

2   It is believed that William Shakespeare was born on April 23, 1564, in Stratford-upon-Avon, though there is no clear documentation verifying that date. Historical evidence shows that Shakespeare was baptized on April 26, and many believe that his birth occurred three days before. Shakespeare's father, John Shakespeare, was variously employed, eventually assuming a position as a town official. His mother, Mary, inherited a great deal of property after the death of her father, allowing the Shakespeare family to live comfortably for some time, though they experienced a number of financial problems in later years. Shakespeare was lucky to have survived into adulthood. Several of his siblings died before they reached their teens, some succumbing to the plague and others dying from other common childhood ailments.

3   It is believed that Shakespeare attended the local public school, possibly ending at the high school level, but there is little documentation to support this theory. It is known that Shakespeare married twenty-six-year-old Anne Hathaway at the age of eighteen. The couple moved to London, where they raised three children. After that, historians note a gap of about seven years in which the activities of the Bard are largely unknown. The next mention of Shakespeare is by Robert Green, a playwright who offered the young writer his first taste of negative criticism in 1592. How and why Shakespeare became involved in the theater is unknown. He seems to have started out as an actor and then had his own plays published. Shakespeare joined the acting troupe the Lord Chamberlain's Men, which was renamed the King's Men after the death of Queen Elizabeth. In this group, Shakespeare sharpened his skills as both an actor and a writer.

4   It is thought that the plays *Two Gentlemen of Verona* and *Love's Labour's Lost* were written during this early period in Shakespeare's career. He would go on to write such well-

known works as *Romeo and Juliet*, *Hamlet* and *Othello*, among others. Of course, besides being a marvelous playwright, Shakespeare was the author of more than a hundred sonnets, many of which are still regarded as literary masterpieces. Eventually, Shakespeare opened the now-famous Globe Theatre in London. The King's Men performed many of the Bard's plays to excited Globe audiences.

5   It is believed that Shakespeare retired from the stage in 1613. The date of his death is, ironically, thought to be April 23, 1616. Shakespeare's works continue to enchant readers everywhere. His stories have a universal quality that has transcended time and space, making Shakespeare literature's most famous and grandest figure.

(?) Questions

7   What does the writer mean by stating that Shakespeare's words "can be found in all four corners of the world"? (paragraph 1)

   A. Shakespeare's plays have been performed in cities around the world.

   B. Shakespeare's works are stored in four different areas.

   C. Shakespeare's words have been published all over the world.

   D. Shakespeare's writings are based on his own world travels.

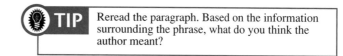

TIP   Reread the paragraph. Based on the information surrounding the phrase, what do you think the author meant?

8   "In this group, Shakespeare sharpened his skills as both an actor and a writer." (paragraph 3)

   Which statement accurately explains the idiom in the sentence from the passage?

   A. Shakespeare taught others how to write.

   B. Shakespeare practiced writing until he got better.

   C. Shakespeare found out that he was not a good writer.

   D. Shakespeare received bad reviews of his writings.

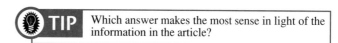

TIP   Which answer makes the most sense in light of the information in the article?

9 In paragraph 5, the author uses the phrase "transcended time and space" to describe Shakespeare's works because

    A. his works reflect various periods throughout history.

    B. new works are still being discovered today.

    C. people still enjoy these works today.

    D. original copies of his works have been found across the globe.

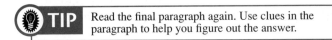

TIP Read the final paragraph again. Use clues in the paragraph to help you figure out the answer.

10 Which sentence describes the effect of the phrases "it is believed" and "it is thought" as they are used in the passage?

    A. They show the uncertainty that surrounds Shakespeare's life.

    B. They depict the inspiration people draw from Shakespeare's work.

    C. They demonstrate that Shakespeare had an unfortunate childhood.

    D. They reinforce the idea that Shakespeare was determined to succeed.

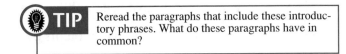

TIP Reread the paragraphs that include these introductory phrases. What do these paragraphs have in common?

Passage 4

Read the following passage. Then answer the questions that follow. Use the Tip below each question to help you choose the correct answer. When you finish, read the answer explanations at the end of this chapter.

Excerpt from "The False Gems"
by Guy de Maupassant

1   Monsieur Lantin had met the young girl at a reception at the house of the second head of his department, and had fallen head over heels in love with her. . . . She and her mother came to live in Paris, where the latter, who made the acquaintance of some of the families in her neighborhood, hoped to find a husband for her daughter.

2   They had very moderate means, and were honorable, gentle, and quiet.

3   The young girl was a perfect type of the virtuous woman in whose hands every sensible young man dreams of one day intrusting his happiness. Her simple beauty had the charm of angelic modesty, and the imperceptible smile which constantly hovered about the lips seemed to be the reflection of a pure and lovely soul.

4   Monsieur Lantin . . . enjoyed a snug little salary of three thousand five hundred francs, and he proposed to this model young girl, and was accepted.

5   She governed his household with such clever economy that they seemed to live in luxury. She lavished the most delicate attentions on her husband, coaxed and fondled him; and so great was her charm that six years after their marriage, Monsieur Lantin discovered that he loved his wife even more than during the first days of their honeymoon.

6   He found fault with only two of her tastes: Her love for the theatre, and her taste for imitation jewelry. Her friends (the wives of some petty officials) frequently procured for her a box at the theatre, often for the first representations of the new plays; and her husband was obliged to accompany her, whether he wished it or not, to these entertainments which bored him excessively after his day's work at the office.

7   After a time, Monsieur Lantin begged his wife to request some lady of her acquaintance to accompany her, and to bring her home after the theatre.

8   Now, with her love for the theatre, came also the desire for ornaments. Her costumes remained as before, simple, in good taste, and always modest; but she soon began to adorn her ears with huge rhinestones, which glittered and sparkled like real diamonds.

9   Her husband frequently remonstrated with her, saying: "My dear, as you cannot afford to buy real jewelry, you ought to appear adorned with your beauty and modesty alone, which are the rarest ornaments of your sex."

10   But she would smile sweetly, and say: "What can I do? I am so fond of jewelry. It is my only weakness. We cannot change our nature."

11   Then she would wind the pearl necklace round her fingers, make the facets of the crystal gems sparkle, and say: "Look! are they not lovely? One would swear they were real."

12   . . . Sometimes, of an evening, when they were enjoying a tete-a-tete by the fireside, she would place on the tea table the morocco leather box containing the "trash," as Monsieur Lantin called it. She would examine the false gems with a passionate attention, as though they imparted some deep and secret joy; and she often persisted in passing a necklace around her husband's neck, and, laughing heartily, would exclaim: "How droll you look!" Then she would throw herself into his arms, and kiss him affectionately.

13   One evening, in winter, she had been to the opera, and returned home chilled through and through. The next morning she coughed, and eight days later she died of inflammation of the lungs.

14   Monsieur Lantin's despair was so great that his hair became white in one month. He wept unceasingly; his heart was broken as he remembered her smile, her voice, every charm of his dead wife.

15   Time did not assuage his grief. . . . Everything in his wife's room remained as it was during her lifetime; all her furniture, even her clothing, being left as it was on the day of her death. Here he was wont to seclude himself daily and think of her who had been his treasure—the joy of his existence.

16   But life soon became a struggle. His income, which, in the hands of his wife, covered all household expenses, was now no longer sufficient for his own immediate wants; and he wondered how she could have managed to buy such excellent wine and the rare delicacies which he could no longer procure with his modest resources. . . .

17   One morning, finding himself without a cent in his pocket, he resolved to sell something, and immediately the thought occurred to him of disposing of his wife's paste jewels,

for he cherished in his heart a sort of rancor against these "deceptions," which had always irritated him in the past. The very sight of them spoiled, somewhat, the memory of his lost darling.

18   To the last days of her life she had continued to make purchases, bringing home new gems almost every evening, and he turned them over some time before finally deciding to sell the heavy necklace, which she seemed to prefer, and which, he thought, ought to be worth about six or seven francs; for it was of very fine workmanship, though only imitation.

19   He put it in his pocket, and started out in search of what seemed a reliable jeweler's shop. At length he found one, and went in, feeling a little ashamed to expose his misery, and also to offer such a worthless article for sale. . . .

20   As soon as the proprietor glanced at the necklace, he cried out: "Ah, parbleu! I know it well; it was bought here."

21   Monsieur Lantin, greatly disturbed, asked: "How much is it worth?"

22   "Well, I sold it for twenty thousand francs. I am willing to take it back for eighteen thousand, when you inform me, according to our legal formality, how it came to be in your possession."

23   This time, Monsieur Lantin was dumfounded. He replied: "But—but—examine it well. Until this moment I was under the impression that it was imitation."

24   The jeweler asked: "What is your name, sir?"

25   "Lantin—I am in the employ of the Minister of the Interior. I live at number sixteen Rue des Martyrs."

26   The merchant looked through his books, found the entry, and said: "That necklace was sent to Madame Lantin's address, sixteen Rue des Martyrs, July 20, 1876."

27   The two men looked into each other's eyes—the widower speechless with astonishment; the jeweler scenting a thief. The latter broke the silence.

28   "Will you leave this necklace here for twenty-four hours?" said he; "I will give you a receipt."

29   Monsieur Lantin answered hastily: "Yes, certainly." Then, putting the ticket in his pocket, he left the store. . . .

30   It must have been a present!—a present!—a present, from whom? Why was it given her? . . . A horrible doubt entered his mind—She? Then, all the other jewels must have been presents, too!

31   The sun awoke him next morning, and he began to dress slowly to go to the office. It was hard to work after such shocks. He sent a letter to his employer, requesting to be excused. Then he remembered that he had to return to the jeweler's. . . . It was a lovely day; a clear, blue sky smiled on the busy city below. Men of leisure were strolling about with their hands in their pockets.

32   Monsieur Lantin, observing them, said to himself: "The rich, indeed, are happy. With money it is possible to forget even the deepest sorrow. . . . Oh if I were only rich!"

33   He perceived that he was hungry, but his pocket was empty. He again remembered the necklace. Eighteen thousand francs! Eighteen thousand francs! What a sum!

34   He soon arrived in the Rue de la Paix, opposite the jeweler's. Eighteen thousand francs! Twenty times he resolved to go in, but shame kept him back. He was hungry, however—very hungry—and not a cent in his pocket. He decided quickly, ran across the street, in order not to have time for reflection, and rushed into the store.

35   The proprietor immediately came forward, and politely offered him a chair; the clerks glanced at him knowingly.

36   "I have made inquiries, Monsieur Lantin," said the jeweler, "and if you are still resolved to dispose of the gems, I am ready to pay you the price I offered."

37   "Certainly, sir," stammered Monsieur Lantin.

38   Whereupon the proprietor took from a drawer eighteen large bills, counted, and handed them to Monsieur Lantin, who signed a receipt; and, with trembling hand, put the money into his pocket.

30   As he was about to leave the store, he turned toward the merchant, who still wore the same knowing smile, and lowering his eyes, said: "I have—I have other gems, which came from the same source. Will you buy them, also?"

40   The merchant bowed: "Certainly, sir."

41   . . . An hour later, he returned with the gems . . . making the sum of one hundred and forty-three thousand francs.

42   The jeweler remarked, jokingly: "There was a person who invested all her savings in precious stones."

43   Monsieur Lantin replied, seriously: "It is only another way of investing one's money."

44   That day he lunched at Voisin's, and drank wine worth twenty francs a bottle. Then he hired a carriage and made a tour of the Bois. He gazed at the various turnouts with a kind of disdain, and could hardly refrain from crying out to the occupants: "I, too, am rich!—I am worth two hundred thousand francs."

45   For the first time in his life, he was not bored at the theatre, and spent the remainder of the night in a gay frolic.

46   Six months afterward, he married again. His second wife was a very virtuous woman; but had a violent temper. She caused him much sorrow.

(?) Questions

11   What does the author mean when he says that Monsieur Lantin "had fallen head over heels" for his wife? (paragraph 1)

   A. He was uncoordinated.

   B. He made very little money.

   C. He cared deeply for his wife.

   D. He was a very intelligent man.

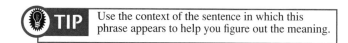

TIP   Use the context of the sentence in which this phrase appears to help you figure out the meaning.

12   In paragraph 12, Monsieur Lantin uses the word *trash* to describe his wife's gems because he thinks that

   A. his wife looks better without them.

   B. they cost too much money.

   C. his wife does not buy him anything nice.

   D. they are gaudy, fake jewelry.

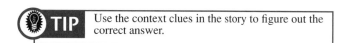

TIP   Use the context clues in the story to figure out the correct answer.

13 Which sentence describes the effect of Monsieur Lantin thinking, "It must have been a present!—a present!—a present, from whom? Why was it given her? . . . A horrible doubt entered his mind—"? (paragraph 30)

  A. He fears that his wife was receiving gifts from another man.

  B. He is angry that his wife spent so much money on the gems.

  C. He suspects that his wife stole the gems from the store.

  D. He is grateful for the money that his wife hid away.

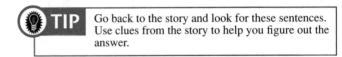

TIP Go back to the story and look for these sentences. Use clues from the story to help you figure out the answer.

14 Identify an example of how irony is used in the story. Write your answer on the lines below.

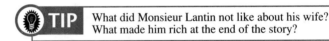

TIP What did Monsieur Lantin not like about his wife? What made him rich at the end of the story?

Answers and Explanations

1   C

'*List* is actually a shortened form of the word *enlist*, and the phrase "off-hand, like" is an idiom meaning "without much thought." This line means that the poet did not give much to enlisting in the military. Answer choice C is correct.

2   B

The poet uses the phrase "quaint and curious" to be sarcastic because he does not really approve of war and feels guilty that he had to kill a man during a war.

3   **Sample answer**

One example of repetition in the poem is the scene of the narrator sitting at an inn or tavern with the man he killed and treating him as a friend. This scene occurs in both the first and last stanzas. Another example is the repetition of the word *foe* in stanza 3. In both cases, the narrator is trying to convince himself that the man he killed was in fact an enemy; however, he cannot get past the fact that under normal circumstances, they would have been friends.

4   **Sample answer**

The narrator describes his mother as "a victim of the system of slavery" to defend his mother for taking the chicken. He explains that the act was not thievery, because the system of slavery had required this action of his mother. Being a slave had changed her to the point that she would do things to survive that she would not have done normally.

5   A

The narrator goes on to compare the children studying in the schoolhouse to paradise. This shows that he was fascinated by the experience.

6   C

Since most people can tell you the exact month, day and year they were born, this sentence reinforces the idea that slaves were considered property, not people. Answer choice C is the correct answer.

7   C

Judging from the information surrounding this sentence, the author is trying to say that Shakespeare's work has been published all over the world.

8   B

The statement that Shakespeare "sharpened his skills" means that he practiced until he got better.

9   C

It is thought that Shakespeare died in 1616, but his works are still studied and enjoyed by people around the world today. This proves that his work has withstood the test of time and space. Answer choice C is correct.

10   A

Phrases such as "it is believed" and "it is thought," which begin nearly every paragraph of the essay, show that the details of Shakespeare's life remain largely unknown and that most of what is known is speculation.

11   C

According to the passage, Monsieur Lantin fell "head over heels" in love with his wife. This is an expression that means he deeply cared about her.

12   D

Throughout the story, we learn that Monsieur Lantin loves everything about his wife except her fake jewelry and her love of the theatre. Answer choice D is correct.

13   A

The jewelry store owner told Monsieur Lantin that the gems were sent to the Lantins' address, which means they were not stolen. Therefore, Monsieur Lantin begins to fear that his wife received the gems as presents, possibly from another man.

14   **Sample answer**

According to the story, Monsieur Lantin did not like his wife's fake jewelry. He called it "trash" and referred to the gems as "paste jewels." It is ironic, however, that the very same jewels that Lantin had always hated turned out to be real gems worth a lot of money. He sold all of them to become rich. The jewels that he thought were cheap costume jewelry ended up making him wealthy.

Chapter 3

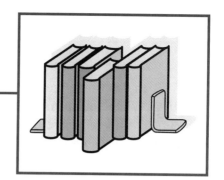

Main Idea, Theme and Supporting Details

Benchmarks

Reading Process: Concepts of Print, Comprehension Strategies and Self-Monitoring Strategies

    A. Apply reading comprehension strategies to understand grade-appropriate text.

Grade Level Indicators

    1 Apply reading comprehension strategies, including making predictions, comparing and contrasting, recalling and summarizing, and making inferences and drawing conclusions.

Reading Applications: Literary Text

    E. Analyze the use of a genre to express a theme or topic.

Grade Level Indicators

    5. Analyze how an author's choice of genre affects the expression of a theme or topic.

Main Idea

The main idea of a passage is what the passage is mostly about. You will be asked to identify the main ideas of passages on the OGT. Main idea questions on the OGT will most often follow nonfiction passages but can follow fiction passages as well.

You can determine the main idea of a passage in several ways. One way is through summarizing. When you **summarize**, you restate a passage, using only the most important ideas and details. This means removing all unnecessary information and including only the essential material, particularly the main idea. Questions on the OGT will ask you to read a passage and then choose a correct summary that states the main idea.

You may also be asked to paraphrase material from a passage. Paraphrasing is similar to summarizing, because it also focuses on the main idea. When you **paraphrase** a sentence, you simply change the wording to reflect your own understanding. When doing this, you need to keep the main idea of the sentence intact.

Theme

Theme is very similar to main idea. The theme of a passage is the overall idea or the message that the work conveys. Some passages may contain more than one theme. Like OGT main idea questions, OGT questions on theme may ask you to choose a statement that best reflects the theme of a passage. If the theme is not stated in the passage, such as in fictional passages or poems, ask yourself what the story or poem is mostly about. Look for symbols that appear continually throughout the work. Sometimes the title can help you find the theme as well. Make sure you choose the answer option that describes the overall idea of the passage. Stay away from options that simply describe a detail.

Supporting Details

A passage will also contain supporting details, which are points that back up or confirm the main idea or theme. For most questions on supporting details, you will find the correct answer by looking back at the passage.

Passage 1

Read the following passage. Then answer the questions that follow. Use the Tip below each question to help you choose the correct answer. When you finish, read the answer explanations at the end of this chapter.

Excerpt from "The Yellow Wallpaper"
by Charlotte Perkins Gilman

1   We have been here two weeks, and I haven't felt like writing before, since that first day. I am sitting by the window now, up in this atrocious nursery, and there is nothing to hinder my writing as much as I please, save lack of strength.

2   John is away all day, and even some nights when his cases are serious. I am glad my case is not serious! But these nervous troubles are dreadfully depressing. John does not know how much I really suffer. He knows there is no REASON to suffer, and that satisfies him.

3   Of course it is only nervousness. It does weigh on me so not to do my duty in any way! I meant to be such a help to John, such a real rest and comfort, and here I am a comparative burden already!

4   Nobody would believe what an effort it is to do what little I am able,—to dress and entertain, and other things. It is fortunate Mary is so good with the baby. Such a dear baby! And yet I CANNOT be with him, it makes me so nervous.

5   I suppose John never was nervous in his life. He laughs at me so about this wall-paper! At first he meant to repaper the room, but afterwards he said that I was letting it get the better of me, and that nothing was worse for a nervous patient than to give way to such fancies.

6   He said that after the wall-paper was changed it would be the heavy bedstead, and then the barred windows, and then that gate at the head of the stairs, and so on. "You know the place is doing you good," he said, "and really, dear, I don't care to renovate the house just for a three months' rental."

7   "Then do let us go downstairs," I said, "there are such pretty rooms there." Then he took me in his arms and called me a blessed little goose, and said he would go down to the cellar, if I wished, and have it whitewashed into the bargain.

8   But he is right enough about the beds and windows and things. It is an airy and comfortable room as any one need wish, and, of course, I would not be so silly as to make him uncomfortable just for a whim. I'm really getting quite fond of the big room, all but that horrid paper. . . .

9   Out of one window I can see the garden, those mysterious deep-shaded arbors, the riotous old-fashioned flowers, and bushes and gnarly trees. Out of another I get a lovely view of the bay and a little private wharf belonging to the estate. There is a beautiful shaded lane that runs down there from the house. I always fancy I see people walking in these numerous paths and arbors, but John has cautioned me not to give way to fancy in the least. He says that with my imaginative power and habit of story-making, a nervous weakness like mine is sure to lead to all manner of excited fancies, and that I ought to use my will and good sense to check the tendency. So I try.

10   I think sometimes that if I were only well enough to write a little it would relieve the press of ideas and rest me. But I find I get pretty tired when I try. It is so discouraging not to have any advice and companionship about my work. When I get really well, John says we will ask Cousin Henry and Julia down for a long visit; but he says he would as soon put fire-works in my pillow-case as to let me have those stimulating people about now. I wish I could get well faster. But I must not think about that. This paper looks to me as if it KNEW what a vicious influence it had!

11   There is a recurrent spot where the pattern lolls like a broken neck and two bulbous eyes stare at you upside down. I get positively angry with the impertinence of it and the ever-lastingness. Up and down and sideways they crawl, and those absurd, unblinking eyes are everywhere. There is one place where two breadths didn't match, and the eyes go all up and down the line, one a little higher than the other. I never saw so much expression in an inanimate thing before, and we all know how much expression they have! I used to lie awake as a child and get more entertainment and terror out of blank walls and plain furniture than most children could find in a toy store. . . .

12   The wall-paper, as I said before, is torn off in spots, and it sticketh closer than a brother—they must have had perseverance as well as hatred. Then the floor is scratched and gouged and splintered, the plaster itself is dug out here and there, and this great heavy bed which is all we found in the room, looks as if it had been through the wars. But I don't mind it a bit—only the paper.

(?) Questions

1   Which of the following themes is supported in the passage?

  A. Women can only be educated in captivity.

  B. Confinement is the worst cure for mental illness.

  C. Women are foolish and must be controlled by men.

  D. Suppression of feminine expression is immoral.

 TIP What is happening in this passage? Read the passage again and look for symbols that may give a hint about its theme.

2   According to the passage, John will not change the wall-paper because

    A. he spends all of his time working on cases.

    B. he thinks it will make the woman more nervous.

    C. the rest of the room is very nicely decorated.

    D. the couple will only live there for a short time.

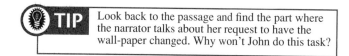

TIP Look back to the passage and find the part where the narrator talks about her request to have the wall-paper changed. Why won't John do this task?

3   "I always fancy I see people walking in these numerous paths and arbors, but John has cautioned me not to give way to fancy in the least. He says that with my imaginative power and habit of story-making, a nervous weakness like mine is sure to lead to all manner of excited fancies, and that I ought to use my will and good sense to check the tendency." (paragraph 9)

Which of the following is the best summary of this excerpt?

    A. The woman believes she sees people outside, but John tells her these visions are imaginary and silly.

    B. John encourages the woman to look out on the paths and arbors and imagine people walking around them.

    C. People enjoy visiting the house to help entertain the woman and John while the woman is recovering.

    D. The woman is afraid she will begin to see things that are not there and invent stories to pass the time.

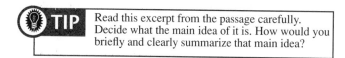

TIP Read this excerpt from the passage carefully. Decide what the main idea of it is. How would you briefly and clearly summarize that main idea?

Passage 2

Read the following passage. Then answer the questions that follow. Use the Tip below each question to help you choose the correct answer. When you finish, read the answer explanations at the end of this chapter.

The Coolest Invention

1   Many parts of the world regularly suffer through severe summer heat. Long ago, much of the United States was considered uninhabitable because of high temperatures. Many kinds of technology have been created since then to make hot climates more comfortable. Primary among these tools is the air conditioner.

2   We may take air conditioners for granted today, but they are very important to many aspects of modern life. Air conditioners not only make our houses cool. They also help factories and businesses run efficiently year-round. They keep food, drinks and medicine fresh and safe. They even protect paper from shrinking and film and paintings from warping.

3   People have tried to build cooling machines for well over a hundred years. The earliest air conditioners were giant pumps that sent dangerous chemicals through pipes. Although these machines did cause some cooling, the toxic, flammable chemicals also resulted in poisonings and fires.

4   The first safe, modern air conditioner was invented by Willis Haviland Carrier in 1902. Just a year after completing his studies as an engineer, Carrier had a "flash of genius." While waiting for a train, he watched the fog and thought about humidity and temperature. By the time the train arrived, Carrier had figured out a formula that would allow a machine to control the temperature.

5   It was in 1902 that Carrier was hired to solve a big problem for a book publisher. The heat and humidity in the printing factory caused the paper to swell. The printers found it difficult to add different-colored inks to the pages because the pages kept warping. Carrier put his "flash of genius" to work and built the first air conditioner. Once installed in the factory, the air conditioner kept the temperature stable. The paper no longer warped. The publishers were thrilled with the device, and Carrier knew he had something special.

6   In 1906, Carrier revealed his perfected machine. The term *air conditioner* didn't catch on until later; at the time, Carrier called his invention the Apparatus for Treating Air. Many industries purchased Carrier's machines, and in 1915, he went into business.

7   Carrier kept on improving his machines for use in factories and businesses. He didn't start thinking about keeping people cool until 1924, when he was asked to install his machines in a department store. Then he installed some in movie theaters. People loved the technology and swarmed to whatever business featured the air-cooling devices.

8   The next great challenge for Carrier was creating an air conditioner that people could use in their homes. In 1928, he designed the Weathermaker, a small, safe household unit. Over the following decades, thousands of people purchased Carrier's machines. Today, air-conditioning is a staple in many homes and businesses—all thanks to Willis Haviland Carrier.

⑦ Questions

4   According to the author, the first cooling machines were unacceptable because

   A. they created a fog.

   B. they heated too quickly.

   C. they were very loud.

   D. they used toxic chemicals.

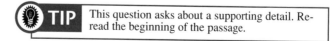

TIP This question asks about a supporting detail. Re-read the beginning of the passage.

5   With which statement would the author probably agree?

  A. Carrier's greatest accomplishment was finding a way to keep department stores cool in the summer.

  B. Carrier's invention allowed people to live in areas once considered inhospitable.

  C. Air-conditioning has not changed at all since the first air conditioner was created by Carrier.

  D. Few people in America use air-conditioning today, and almost nobody relies on it.

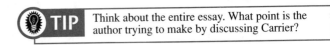

TIP   Think about the entire essay. What point is the author trying to make by discussing Carrier?

6   Summarize paragraph 5. Write your answer on the lines below.

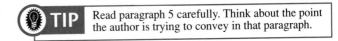

TIP   Read paragraph 5 carefully. Think about the point the author is trying to convey in that paragraph.

7   The passage indicates that Carrier was inspired to create the first air conditioner because of

  A. the work of other inventors.

  B. extensive trial and error.

  C. observations of nature.

  D. the severe heat in his home.

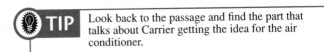

TIP   Look back to the passage and find the part that talks about Carrier getting the idea for the air conditioner.

Passage 3

Read the following passage. Then answer the questions that follow. Use the Tip below each question to help you choose the correct answer. When you finish, read the answer explanations at the end of this chapter.

The Thinking Spot

1   It was a Saturday afternoon and I was supposed to be writing a journal entry for Monday's English class about my fondest childhood memory. Unfortunately, the rhythmic blinking of the cursor was the only movement on my otherwise blank computer screen. Frustrated, I let my eyes wander to the window. The mammoth oak tree in my backyard dominated most of the view. Fresh leaves the vivid green of spring fluttered in the breeze, and the old swing that hung from the tree's largest branch gently swayed back and forth. "My thinking spot," I said aloud. Leaving all thoughts of homework assignments behind, I went outside.

2   I circled the old swing several times, tugging the ropes to make sure they weren't rotted and rubbing my hand across the wooden seat to check for splinters. Determining it safe for use, I hoisted myself onto the seat and pumped my legs back and forth. Though it had probably been six or seven years since my last outing on the swing, the pendulum-like motion felt familiar and comfortable. I remembered why this had once been my favorite location to sit and contemplate the world. As the swing traveled back and forth, my mind opened and thoughts deluged my brain.

3   Suddenly, I was five years old again, begging my grandpa to push me on the swing. "C'mon, Gramp," I would plead, adding the one phrase I knew he couldn't resist: "Pretty please with a cherry on top." Whether it was the missing front tooth in my awkward smile or the unraveling braids of my brown hair, Gramp would grin and crumble and I would have my way. Within minutes, we would traipse hand-in-hand across the dew-covered lawn toward the swing.

4   "Hold on tight," he would say, as he gave the swing a hefty push to get it started. I would smile and giggle as the swing flew higher and higher into the air. Soon, I could see over the Millers' fence, right into their pool, and catch a glimpse of the football stuck in the Carmichaels' gutter. I could see the patch of shingles on the roof of my house where Dad had patched a leak during a rainstorm. Wispy strands of hair would fly away from my face, and then tickle my cheeks and forehead as the swing moved forward and backward.

5   As darkness fell, Gramp would slow the swing to a stop and lift me onto his shoulders. We would return to the house, following the dim glow cast from the kitchen window. Once inside, Gramp would settle into an armchair, I would climb into his lap and he would read me a book of children's poems by Robert Louis Stevenson. When he reached my favorite rhyme, I would recite it right along with him: "Oh how I love to go up in a swing. . . ."

6   When Gramp wasn't around, sometimes I could convince my older brother, George, to push me on the swing. George's technique was much different than Gramp's. Instead of starting out slow and allowing the swing to steadily fly higher and higher, George would pull the swing as far back and as high as he could—sometimes I felt like I might slip right out of the seat!—and then he would run, full speed, right underneath the swing. "Underdog!" he would yell as he released the ropes, and I would shriek with a combination of excited delight and fear that I would swing upside-down, right over the tree branch.

7   By the time I was nine years old, Gramp had moved into a nursing home, and George had gotten his driver's license and wasn't home much. It was up to me to get my swing moving faster and higher, and to create my own thrilling adventures. In my mind, my swing had been my spaceship, rocketing around the universe at record speeds, and my Pegasus, the flying horse of Greek mythology. It had been my trapeze, my time machine and the dragon I had tamed as the world's fiercest female knight. But most of all, my swing had been my "thinking spot," the one place where I knew I could completely lose myself in thought. Riding my swing, I must have composed thousands of songs and poems, and hundreds of scenarios for my friends and me to act out.

8   That Saturday on the swing was no different. As I scuffed my feet through the worn patch of grass beneath the swing and gradually came to a stop, I felt as though I had accomplished the impossible. Returning to my computer, my fingers danced across the keyboard and I watched as the screen filled with the fondest memory from my childhood: my thinking spot.

(?) Questions

8   From reading paragraph 2, you can infer that the swing

   A. was made of simple materials.

   B. was not strong enough to be safe.

   C. had been built far from the house.

   D. had been used by many children.

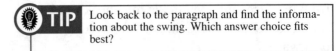

TIP Look back to the paragraph and find the information about the swing. Which answer choice fits best?

9   "In my mind, my swing had been my spaceship, rocketing around the universe at record speeds, and my Pegasus, the flying horse of Greek mythology. It had been my trapeze, my time machine and the dragon I had tamed as the world's fiercest female knight. But most of all, my swing had been my 'thinking spot,' the one place where I knew I could completely lose myself in thought." (paragraph 7)

Which of the following is the best summary of this excerpt?

A. The swing reminded the author of a Pegasus, a dragon, a time machine, a trapeze and a spaceship.

B. The author had a wild imagination, which must have helped her create many songs and poems.

C. Dragons and flying horses are popular creatures in many children's daydreams.

D. The author created many stories about her swing, but it served her best as a spot where she could think.

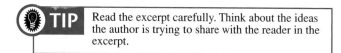

TIP   Read the excerpt carefully. Think about the ideas the author is trying to share with the reader in the excerpt.

10   Summarize paragraph 1. Write your answer on the lines below.

_____

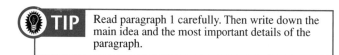

TIP   Read paragraph 1 carefully. Then write down the main idea and the most important details of the paragraph.

11   "As the swing traveled back and forth, my mind opened and thoughts deluged my brain." (paragraph 7)

This sentence from paragraph 2 can be paraphrased by which of the following statements?

A. The motion of the swing helped me get new ideas.

B. I constantly thought about other places I'd rather be.

C. As I began to swing, I injured my head.

D. For a long time, I thought about how much fun swings are.

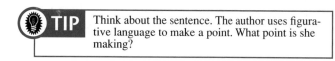

TIP   Think about the sentence. The author uses figurative language to make a point. What point is she making?

Passage 4

Read the following passage. Then answer the questions that follow. Use the Tip below each question to help you choose the correct answer. When you finish, read the answer explanations at the end of this chapter.

John Mercer Langston: Ohio Abolitionist

1 Most people have heard of Martin Luther King Jr., Frederick Douglass and Harriet Tubman. These civil rights leaders dedicated their lives to reforming America's perspectives on race relations and improving the lives of African Americans. Many more civil rights pioneers are not as commonly studied, however. Among them is John Mercer Langston, who helped break barriers for black people in his home state of Ohio and, ultimately, throughout the country.

2 John Mercer Langston was born in Virginia in 1829. Although slavery was legal in Virginia at that time, Langston was born free. His father was a wealthy plantation owner, and his mother was a former slave who had been freed, or emancipated. When Langston was only five years old, both of his parents died and he inherited a considerable amount of money.

3 As a young man, Langston moved to Cincinnati, Ohio, where he found an active community of African Americans. Ohio was a free state, meaning that slavery was outlawed there, but black residents still felt the sting of prejudice. They helped one another endure their problems, and they warmly welcomed Langston when he arrived in the city.

4 When he was only fourteen, Langston enrolled in Oberlin College's Preparatory Department. He proved to be a dedicated student with a great flare for debate. After six years of education at Oberlin, Langston became the school's fifth African American graduate. More importantly, through his time in Cincinnati and his education at Oberlin, Langston had chosen his life's goal: He would strive to promote the rights of black Americans.

5 In 1848, John Mercer Langston combined his talent for debate with his enthusiasm for civil rights. As a guest of the famous abolitionist Frederick Douglass, Langston gave a speech at Cleveland's National Black Convention. In his first public appearance, Langston deftly argued against slavery and showed his support for citizens who aided others in escaping slavery. Langston did not confine his work to study and lectures, though; he organized antislavery groups and even participated in the Underground Railroad, which assisted slaves from southern states in escaping into the North.

6 During this time, Langston continued his education, studying law at Oberlin and Elyria. In 1854, he became Ohio's first black lawyer and established a law practice in Brownhelm, Ohio, where he settled down with his wife, Caroline Wall. Langston proved a success-

ful and well-respected mainstay of the community. When he was elected to be Brownhelm's town clerk, Langston became the first African American in history to be elected to a public office.

7   Langston remained in politics for some time, serving in various capacities but always spreading his antislavery ideals. Although he was popular and his ideas were embraced by many, Langston was not satisfied with the slow progress of the abolitionists. He explored several different ideas of ridding the country of slavery. When the Civil War began in 1861, he worked quickly to organize America's first black regiment. Although he wanted to personally lead such a regiment into battle, the war ended before he could gain the support he needed to do so.

8   Langston's civilian contributions were just as important. He began focusing on bringing suffrage—the right to vote—and education to all Americans. A few years after the war ended, he had helped sway Congress to pass laws allowing black men to vote. Meanwhile, Langston's work to bring educational equality was well received. More and more universities began opening their doors to blacks and to women thanks to Langston's compelling arguments for human equality.

9   Later in his life, Langston served as a university president, an overseas ambassador and even a member of the House of Representatives. When he died in 1897, thousands mourned his death. However, John Mercer Langston's pioneering work and words live on and continue to inspire people to this day.

⁇ Questions

12 Which sentence summarizes paragraph 7?

   A. Langston opposed slavery in many ways, including organizing a black regiment in the Civil War.

   B. Langston tried to gain the support he needed to lead soldiers into battle in the Civil War.

   C. The first regiment of black soldiers in American history was organized during the Civil War.

   D. The Civil War began in 1861 and the slavery question became crucial throughout America.

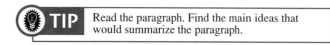

TIP	Read the paragraph. Find the main ideas that would summarize the paragraph.

13 What is a plausible theme for this passage? Support your answer with an example from the passage. Write your answer on the lines below.

_____

 TIP Think about what you know of themes. What important concept, or theme, is best linked to this passage?

14 Which subheading accurately reflects the information in paragraph 5?

   A. Langston's Lifelong Education

   B. New Neighbors in Cincinnati

   C. Antislavery Words and Deeds

   D. The Underground Railroad

 TIP Read paragraph 5, and then think about the most important idea or ideas in the paragraph.

Answers and Explanations

1   C

In Victorian times, women were thought to be foolish. The story suggests that the narrator's husband controlled her life and even imprisoned her in the hopes of curing her of her nervous ideas and behaviors, which he thinks are silly.

2   D

The narrator explains that John does not want to change the wall-paper because the couple will only live in the home for three months.

3   A

John discourages the narrator from her visions, believing them to be silly and imaginary.

4   D

Early cooling machines used chemicals that were dangerous and poisonous.

5   B

According to the passage, many areas in America were considered almost uninhabitable before air conditioners allowed people to live comfortably in high temperatures.

6   Sample answer

Carrier first created an air conditioner when he was hired to solve a big problem for a book publisher. The heat and humidity in the printing factory made the paper swell and the pages warp. Carrier created an air conditioner to solve that problem.

7   C

In paragraph 4, the author explains that Carrier got the idea for the air conditioner while waiting for a train and watching the fog in the air.

8   A

Paragraph 2 mentions that the swing is made of a piece of wood and old ropes. You can infer that these are simple materials.

9   D

This excerpt explains the many things that the author daydreamed about her swing. These details make the story interesting but are unimportant to the main idea. The main idea is that she had many ideas about the swing and the swing helped her think.

10 **Sample answer**

On a Saturday afternoon, the author tried unsuccessfully to write a journal entry about a childhood memory. After looking out the window and seeing her old swing swaying from a branch in the huge oak tree in her yard, however, she remembered that that was her "thinking spot." She goes there to find inspiration.

11 A

The author says that her "mind opened and thoughts deluged [her] brain." This means that the swinging motion helped her to think and flooded her brain with ideas.

12 A

Paragraph 7 explains Langston's frustration with the slow progress of the abolitionists and says he tried many ideas, including organizing a black regiment.

13 **Sample answer**

A theme of this passage may be that brave and thoughtful individuals can help to change history. The passage is all about a man who breaks traditional barriers and proves that African Americans deserve the same rights as other people. This one man made great positive changes in America.

14 C

Paragraph 5 begins by explaining how Langston first used words to argue against slavery, and it goes on to describe some of his antislavery deeds.

Chapter 4

Evaluating Information

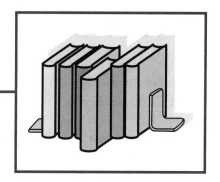

Benchmarks

Reading Process: Concepts of Print, Comprehension Strategies and Self-Monitoring Strategies

    A. Apply reading comprehension strategies to understand grade-appropriate text.

    B. Demonstrate comprehension of print and electronic text by responding to questions (e.g., literal, inferential, evaluative and synthesizing).

Grade Level Indicators

    1. Apply reading comprehension strategies, including making predictions, comparing and contrasting, recalling and summarizing, and making inferences and drawing conclusions.

    2. Answer literal, inferential, evaluative and synthesizing questions to demonstrate comprehension of grade-appropriate print texts and electronic and visual media.

How Do You Evaluate Information?

To answer questions on the OGT assessed by this benchmark, you will need to read the information in passages carefully and show that you understand the information in them. You might have to analyze or synthesize information. When you **synthesize** information, you process it, meaning you completely understand it and can use it in a different situation.

    On the OGT, you may be asked to recall details from a passage or to summarize information in a passage. A **summary** is a brief statement that presents the main ideas of a passage in a concise form. To answer some questions, you will have to make an inference or conclusion. **Inferences** and **conclusions** are guesses based on known facts or premises.

Many questions for this benchmark will ask you to apply what you have learned from reading a passage. You might have to draw a conclusion based on the text. Some questions on the OGT will ask you about the literal or inferential meaning of an element of the passage. A **literal meaning** is one that you do not have to interpret; it is the essential or explicit meaning of an idea or statement. Questions on literal meaning will ask you about the information stated in the text. An **inferential meaning** is one that is implied and thus requires your interpretation; it is the indirect meaning of an idea or statement. For questions on inferential meaning, you may be asked to restate an idea or line in a passage. You may also be asked to describe why a character in a fictional passage has behaved in a certain way.

Some questions on this benchmark will require you to evaluate the information you have read in a passage. **Evaluating** information might require you to judge the value, significance or worth of information in a passage or a statement made by an author or character in a story.

You might also be asked to compare and contrast ideas or information in a passage. When you **compare and contrast**, you identify how things are alike and different. Comparison questions ask you how two things are alike; contrast questions ask you how two things are different.

Although you will often be able to find the answers to compare and contrast questions right in the text, at other times you will have to synthesize or analyze information to find the right answers. Compare and contrast questions usually include words and phrases such as *alike, different, like, similar, the major advantage/disadvantage, the major difference between* and *the most important difference.*

For fiction passages on the OGT, you may be asked to compare or contrast two characters in a short story or in two different stories or poems. You might also be asked to compare and contrast the setting, tone or topic of two works of fiction. Some questions will ask you why the author compares things, ideas or people. These questions often contain similes (comparisons using *like* or *as*) or metaphors (comparisons in which one thing stands for another).

For nonfiction passages, you might be asked to compare and contrast the main idea, author's purpose or point of view. You might also be asked to compare and contrast supporting details about a subject, such as what is alike or different about something.

Some questions on the OGT will ask you to make predictions. When you make a prediction, you guess what might happen in the future based on what you have learned about a situation.

Questions for this benchmark will be multiple choice, short response or extended response. Passages will be either fiction or nonfiction.

Passage 1

Read the following passage. Then answer the questions that follow. Use the Tip below each question to help you choose the correct answer. When you finish, read the answer explanations at the end of this chapter.

Safe at Sixteen? Why We Should Raise the Legal Driving Age
by Eliot Golden

1   To many teens, turning sixteen is a rite of passage. In most states, this is the age when young people can apply for a driver's license. Teens see this as the beginning of freedom and independence. They think it is a time to enjoy being young and carefree. Though many teens feel excited about being able to drive, many adults feel that this is a dangerous and sometimes deadly time for young drivers. Their fears are confirmed by some scary statistics. Studies show that young drivers are more likely to speed, run red lights and drive recklessly than more mature, experienced drivers.

2   Many experts agree that this kind of behavior accounts for the thousands of teens killed every year in automobile accidents. In fact, according to the National Center for Injury Prevention and Control, teens are four times more likely to crash than older drivers. This has caused many to question what can be done to keep teen drivers safe.

3   A growing number of people feel that the only way to truly prevent tragedy is to raise the legal driving age. Most teens, and even some parents, scoff at this idea. However, many people feel that this is necessary. Some of our nation's lawmakers agree. A number of states have already raised the minimum age a teen must be to acquire a full, unrestricted license. This means that many young drivers can only drive with a licensed adult in the car. These states use graduated licensing programs that put limitations on young drivers. The programs restrict teens from driving late at night or carrying other teenage passengers until they have logged a certain number of hours driving under the supervision of a parent or guardian. Safety experts point out that more supervised experience makes safer drivers and reduces the risk of fatal accidents among teens. But are these programs doing enough to keep kids safe?

4   Researchers also note that maturity plays a major role in safety on the roads. Many young drivers are overconfident in their abilities. They don't think about the risks associated with getting behind the wheel. Studies show that out of all age groups, teens are the most likely to drive while under the influence of alcohol or drugs. They are also the most likely to drive without wearing seat belts and to underestimate the dangers of hazardous road conditions. Some argue that making mature decisions about driving is something that can only come with age. These people feel that the number of hours young drivers spend practicing does not matter.

5   Keeping all this in mind, the only logical and responsible solution to the problem is to raise the legal driving age. Many teens will argue that their freedom is being taken from them.

Many parents might be inconvenienced by having to drive their kids to school, work or practice. But the alternative is far worse! Turning sixteen is an important milestone in any young person's life, but it doesn't necessarily mean that he or she is ready to drive. By raising the legal driving age and giving teens more time and experience behind the wheel, we can help make sure that turning seventeen, eighteen and nineteen is just as exciting and safe for teens.

⑦ Questions

1   Unlike other drivers, teenagers are

   A. usually under the influence while driving.

   B. four times more likely to be involved in a car crash.

   C. using caution when they get behind the wheel.

   D. mature enough to handle many dangerous situations.

 This question asks you to recall a detail from the passage. Take another look at paragraph 2. The author explains the differences between teenage drivers and older drivers. Consider each option before choosing an answer.

2   Which sentence summarizes paragraph 4?

   A. Most teens do not practice driving.

   B. Young drivers are not confident.

   C. Most teens do not wear seat belts.

   D. Young drivers tend to be careless.

 This is a summary question. It asks you to choose the statement that presents the main ideas of paragraph 4 in a brief form. Some of these choices may present details from the paragraph but may not represent the main idea of the entire paragraph. Which choice is a summary of the paragraph?

3   Which sentence summarizes the purpose of paragraphs 1 and 2 in the passage?

   A. They convince readers that the driving age should be raised.

   B. They establish the need for a change in the driving laws.

   C. They indicate that most teens are good, safe drivers.

   D. They specify which driving laws keep teens the safest.

 This is a different kind of summary question. This question asks you to consider why the author has set up the information in the passage the way he has. What do you think these paragraphs have been designed to do? What is their purpose?

Passage 2

Read the following passage. Then answer the questions that follow. Use the Tip below each question to help you choose the correct answer. When you finish, read the answer explanations at the end of this chapter.

American Aid Essential for First-Rate Foreign Relations

Glorytown Gazette

Letters to the Editor

1   To the Editor:

2   I am writing in response to a letter that appeared in yesterday's newspaper. In the letter, Edwin Stanton stated that the United States should not be providing financial aid to foreign countries. Mr. Stanton feels that our government should not give away its citizens' hard-earned tax money, no matter what the cause. He stated that "each nation should be responsible for standing on its own two feet," and that "America should not help poor people of other nations when there is so much poverty at home." Although I believe that a couple of the points in Mr. Stanton's letter are valid, most are based on misconceptions. I hope that the majority of my fellow citizens do not share his severe views—or we may someday be in trouble and find ourselves with nowhere to turn.

3   One of the main goals of the American government in handing out aid to foreign nations is to increase the potential for worldwide democracy. It seems that nations under a dictatorship are far less likely to conduct positive foreign relations with the United States than those with a democratic government. By providing money—and other types of aid—to foreign countries, America can secure peaceful relations with those countries and create political and military alliances that may help us in the future. By aiding others, we ultimately aid ourselves as well.

4   I do not think that Mr. Stanton understands the figures in this debate, either. Foreign aid represents less than 1 percent of America's budget. This is hardly an enormous waste of taxpayer dollars, as Mr. Stanton seems to believe. Many other countries—Japan, Sweden, the Netherlands and Denmark, to name a few—expend a larger percentage of their gross national product (the total value of goods and services produced by the residents of a nation during a specified period) in financing foreign aid than the United States does. Furthermore, many other countries have offered help to us in times of need, including Cuba and Venezuela, with whom international relations have been somewhat strained at times.

5   I just hope that people who read Mr. Stanton's letter think about these points as well and refrain from adopting his ideas. If we all thought as he does, the world would never change.

6   Kat McClanahan

7   Glorytown, USA

⑦ Questions

4   In paragraph 3, the passage declares, "By aiding others, we ultimately aid ourselves as well."

How does the letter writer feel America helps itself in giving foreign aid?

A. by charging foreign countries high-interest on loans

B. by establishing good relationships with potential allies

C. by showing other countries how powerful we are

D. by contributing money to the international economy

 TIP This question asks you to recall a detail from the passage. Reread paragraph 3. What does the author mean when she makes this point? Which answer choice represents the author's views?

5   According to the passage, what should Americans do if a dictatorship needs help?

A. investigate what was done in the past

B. encourage them to change their ways

C. give them help without question

D. consider giving help to the country

 TIP This question asks you to predict what type of action the country might take based on the information in the passage. Reread the third paragraph of the passage. What does the author say about giving to dictatorships?

6   Which sentence summarizes the purpose of paragraph 4 in the passage?

A. It proves that America should not give money to certain countries.

B. It points out that America has given aid to many countries.

C. It shows that foreign aid is a small part of the country's budget.

D. It mentions countries with which relations have been strained.

 TIP Some of these answer choices may represent points that have been made in the paragraph, and some may misrepresent information found in the paragraph. However, only one choice represents the main idea of the paragraph. Which choice is the best summary of the information in this paragraph?

Passage 3

Read the following passage. Then answer the questions that follow. Use the Tip below each question to help you choose the correct answer. When you finish, read the answer explanations at the end of this chapter.

Lively Lizards

The Colorful Chameleon

1   Wild chameleons live in very few places in the world. Those that are housed as pets in the United States and other places on the continent were shipped from Madagascar, India, Yemen, Kenya or South Africa. About half of the world's chameleon population, which totals about 135 species, can be found in Madagascar, an island off the coast of Africa. In fact, Madagascar is the only place to find 59 of the world's chameleon species, including the largest, the Parson's chameleon, which can grow to be the size of a cat.

2   Chameleons are known for their ability to change the color of their skin. Most people believe that chameleons change color to blend in with their surroundings; however, this is a widespread misconception about these lizards. Chameleons change color according to temperature or mood or to communicate with other chameleons. They do not have an unlimited array of skin colors but can exhibit shades of green, brown, red, blue, yellow, white or black.

3   Although many chameleons normally appear to be green or brown, the outer layer of skin is actually transparent. The layers of skin cells underneath are where pigments called chromatophores and melanin are located. These cells expand and contract depending on a chameleon's body temperature or mood. If a chameleon is too warm, its brain will tell the lighter-colored skin cells to enlarge so that it can reflect light off its body rather than absorbing it. Bright colors are used to attract mates, and dark colors are used to show enemies that the chameleon is ready to attack, if necessary. In self-defense, a chameleon might also hiss and spring at its would-be attacker.

4   Despite the constant danger of being eaten by snakes or birds, the greatest threat to chameleons is the human race. When trees are cut down to create farmlands, fuel for heat or housing materials, the arboreal chameleon has nowhere to live and must seek out a new habitat. Some chameleons adapt well to these changes and successfully discover new dwellings. Others do not fare as well. Agricultural chemicals can also kill off these likable creatures.

Another—perhaps greater—threat to chameleon populations is their export for sale in America and other countries. Almost 100,000 chameleons are shipped out of their countries of origin every year. Some are not equipped to survive the transport, and others will not adapt to the North American climate. The ones that do survive the trip are sold in pet stores or on the Internet. Many countries are working to pass laws banning chameleon export, allowing chameleons to live and thrive on their native lands.

❓ Questions

7   The purpose of paragraph 2 in the passage is to

    A. correct a popular misunderstanding.

    B. demonstrate the author's knowledge of chameleons.

    C. warn readers that chameleons frequently attack.

    D. stop people from exporting chameleons.

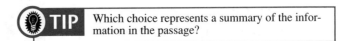

TIP Which choice represents a summary of the information in the passage?

8   Which statement accurately describes chameleons according to the article and the photographs?

    A. Chameleons are often pink or orange.

    B. Chameleons live well in captivity.

    C. Chameleons vary in size and shape.

    D. Chameleons adapt well to change.

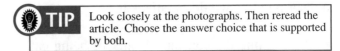

TIP Look closely at the photographs. Then reread the article. Choose the answer choice that is supported by both.

9   What behavior might be exhibited by a chameleon living in a brightly lit tank?

   A. It might hiss and spring at the glass.

   B. It might lighten the color of its skin.

   C. It might communicate with other chameleons.

   D. It might blend in with its surroundings.

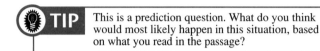

TIP This is a prediction question. What do you think would most likely happen in this situation, based on what you read in the passage?

10   What are some reasons chameleons should be left in their native habitat and not exported to the United States? Support your answer with examples from the passage.

_____

TIP Reread the end of the article. Jot down some reasons why people are trying to get laws passed to prevent the export of chameleons to the United States.

Passage 4

Read the following passage. Then answer the questions that follow. Use the Tip below each question to help you choose the correct answer. When you finish, read the answer explanations at the end of this chapter.

Carbohydrate Craze

Carb-Free Is Unhealthy

by Dr. Rubina Gad

1   The American public's obsession with dieting has led to one of the most dangerous health misconceptions of all time. Many television ads, sitcoms, movies, magazine articles and diet-food product labels would have consumers believe that carbohydrates are bad for the human body and that those who eat them will quickly become overweight. We are advised to avoid foods such as pasta, potatoes, rice and white bread and opt for meats and vegetables instead. Some companies promote this idea to encourage consumers to buy their "carb-free" food products. But the truth is, as I stress to patients who come to our weight-loss clinic, the human body needs carbohydrates to function properly, and a body that is starved of this dietary element is not in good shape after all.

2   Carbohydrates are macronutrients, meaning they are essential sources of fuel that are necessary for survival. Contrary to popular belief, carbohydrates have many health benefits; however, the key to maintaining a healthy body is to consume these and other macronutrients—such as protein and fat—in appropriate amounts.

3   Most foods that we consume on a daily basis are loaded with carbohydrates. Many people mistakenly believe that carbohydrates can only be found in filling foods such as potatoes and pastas. In truth, carbohydrates are also naturally found in fruits, vegetables, dairy products and whole grains. Many of these carbohydrate-containing foods also have essential health benefits; some fight diseases such as high blood pressure and heart disease, and others help to prevent cancer and stroke. Cutting these foods out of your diet may increase your chances of contracting one of these diseases. It also deprives your body of the many health benefits of carbohydrates.

4   One of the best benefits of carbohydrates is their ability to provide fuel to the muscles and the brain. They also help to maintain the health of our organs, tissues and cells. Scientific studies have shown that one type of carbohydrate called fiber, also commonly referred to as roughage, reduces the risk of heart disease and diabetes. Carbohydrates also contain antioxidants, which protect the body's cells from harmful particles with the potential to cause cancer.

5   This does not mean that the human body can survive on a diet composed entirely of carbohydrates. We also need certain percentages of proteins and fats to maintain healthy bodies. But carbohydrates certainly should not be avoided altogether. In fact, the food pyramid, the recommended basis for a healthy diet, shows that a person should consume six to eleven servings of breads, grains and pastas, as well as three to four servings each of fruits and vegetables—all carbohydrate-containing foods. It is easy to see why cutting carbohydrates out of a person's diet is not a good idea.

6   The only way to know what is truly healthy for your own body is to talk to a nutritionist or dietitian, who can help you choose foods that are right for you as well as guide you toward a proper exercise program for weight loss, muscle gain or toning. These professionals will never tell you to cut out carbohydrates entirely. The bottom line: listen to the experts, not the advertisers!

Questions

11 According to the author, which is an effect of cutting carbohydrates out of your diet?

   A. Your risk of heart disease and diabetes will decrease.

   B. Your body will miss getting many antioxidants.

   C. You will lower your chances of having a stroke.

   D. Your body will get in much better shape.

> **TIP** This question tests your reading comprehension. It asks you to recall a detail that you learned while reading the passage. Read the passage again. Which statement describes an effect of cutting carbohydrates out of your diet?

12 Which of these subtitles might be an appropriate alternative to the one already used for this article?

   A. A Matter of Proper Proportions

   B. Kinds of Carb-Free Foods

   C. A Weight-Loss Case Study

   D. Exercise the Excess Away

 This question asks you to make an inference or conclusion. Look at each subtitle. Based on what you know about the information in the passage, which subtitle do you think would fit with one of the paragraphs in the passage?

13 Which quote illustrates the author's use of compare-and-contrast organization?

   A. "One of the best benefits of carbohydrates is their ability to provide fuel to the muscles and the brain."

   B. "It is easy to see why cutting carbohydrates out of a person's diet is not a good idea."

   C. "But carbohydrates certainly should not be avoided altogether."

   D. "Contrary to popular belief, carbohydrates have many health benefits."

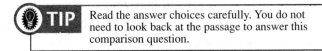 Read the answer choices carefully. You do not need to look back at the passage to answer this comparison question.

14 The title of the article, "Carbohydrate Craze: Carb-Free Is Unhealthy," suggests that cutting carbohydrates out of a person's diet can be harmful to that person's health. The author of the article supports this idea by offering examples of how carbohydrates are good for people. Explain some of the benefits of carbohydrates. Support your explanation with three examples or details from the passage.

 Reread the article. Jot down the reasons carbohydrates are good for you, and then review your notes before composing your response.

Answers and Explanations

1   B

The passage states that teenage drivers are four times more likely to be involved in a car crash than older drivers.

2   D

The main idea of the paragraph is that young drivers tend to be careless when they are behind the wheel.

3   B

The purpose of information in these paragraphs is to set up or establish the need to change the driving laws. The paragraphs present the problems and safety concerns surrounding young drivers, which lets the readers know why the author is making this argument.

4   B

The author makes the point that providing other countries with money helps America establish good relationships with those countries and gives America international friends to call on in tough times if need be.

5   C

The author says the United States should give to these countries to improve its relations with them.

6   C

The author makes the point that Mr. Stanton does not understand the figures in the debate. She proves this by making the point that America does not spend nearly as much on foreign aid as Mr. Stanton has suggested.

7   A

The author explains that chameleons do not change color to blend in with their surroundings, which is a widely held misconception.

8   C

You can tell from the photographs and from the article that there are many kinds of chameleons.

9   B

The passage states that if a chameleon is too warm, its brain will enlarge its lighter-colored skin cells so that it can reflect light off its body rather than absorbing it.

10 **Sample answer**

Chameleons are better off left in their native lands, because the climate suits them well. Some chameleons exported to the United States are not equipped to survive transportation. Others simply cannot adapt to the change in climate. That is why people are trying to pass laws banning chameleon exportation.

11 B

The passage explains that carbohydrates contain antioxidants. Without carbohydrates, a person's body is deprived of the antioxidants that carbohydrates normally provide.

12 A

The fifth paragraph of the article explains that our bodies need certain proportions of a variety of food elements in order to stay healthy. The other choices describe topics either not discussed in the passage or not discussed in detail in the passage.

13 D

This choice contrasts popular opinion and the truth. The word contrary lets readers know that a contrast is being made.

14 **Sample answer**

Carbohydrates are good for people in many different ways. In the article, Dr. Gad tells readers that carbohydrates provide our muscles and brain with the fuel they need to function. Without fuel, our muscles and brain would not operate properly. She also explains that carbohydrates help keep our organs, tissues and cells in good shape. This is an essential aspect of maintaining total health. Dr. Gad tells us that consuming carbohydrates helps to reduce our risks for diseases such as heart disease, diabetes and cancer. These are all reasons why carbohydrates are an essential and healthy part of a balanced diet.

Chapter 5

Author's Purpose

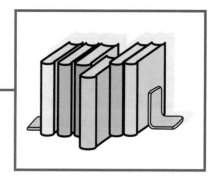

Benchmarks

Reading Applications: Informational, Technical and Persuasive Text

B. Identify examples of rhetorical devices and valid and invalid inferences, and explain how authors use these devices to achieve their purposes and reach their intended audiences.

D. Explain and analyze how an author appeals to an audience and develops an argument or viewpoint in text.

Grade Level Indicators

4. Assess the adequacy, accuracy and appropriateness of an author's details, identifying persuasive techniques (e.g., bandwagon, testimonial, transfer, glittering generalities, emotional word repetition, bait and switch) and examples of propaganda, bias and stereotyping.

5. Analyze an author's implicit and explicit argument, perspective or viewpoint in text.

6. Identify appeals to authority, reason and emotion.

8. Identify the features of rhetorical devices used in common types of public documents, including newspaper editorials and speeches.

Why Do Authors Write?

Authors write for various reasons. Some write short stories, novels or poems to entertain their readers. Other authors write articles or nonfiction books to inform or describe something to readers. Still others write political speeches, editorial opinion pieces or letters to editors to persuade readers to think and act as they do about certain issues.

The OGT includes questions about authors' purposes. Some questions will ask you to describe the effect of an author's word choices. Others will ask you about an author's opinion or point of view. For example, you might have to determine how an author feels about his or her subject matter. In addition, you might have to determine why an author writes a certain way. For example, you might be asked why an author asks a question at the beginning of an essay. Another question you are likely to see on the OGT will ask you to identify a statement that an author would likely support; to answer this type of question, you will need to determine an author's opinion of the topic at hand.

Passage 1

Read the following passage. Then answer the questions that follow. Use the Tip below each question to help you choose the correct answer. When you finish, read the answer explanations at the end of this chapter.

Unwinding Our Minds

The Ohioans' Voice

Letters to the Editor

1   Dear Editor:

2   People today seem to be more vulnerable to stress than ever before. In the slow-paced world of the past, people were content to loll around after dinner, talking until the sun went down, signaling the end of the day. This world no longer exists; our days do not end at sundown, and many of us feel both societal and personal pressure to limit our leisure time.

3   One reason for this phenomenon is the technological advances that make it possible to contact anyone, anywhere, anytime. Work no longer ends when we leave our offices; it can continue long into the night if we allow ourselves to keep going. Research can be conducted from home without setting foot inside a library, making it easier to keep working and harder to relax.

4   Another reason we are so stressed is that our current world is filled with multitasking, both at home and at work. While women and men of the past occupied separate and distinct roles, today's men and women fill the historical tasks of both genders at once. Our busy lives cause our minds to work overtime, leading to tension, sleeplessness, extreme fatigue and more serious health problems such as heart disease and high blood pressure.

5   However, not everyone has fallen into the trap of modern stressors. Many people find time to unwind through a variety of relaxation methods. Yoga provides us with a way to relax the body and mind through stretching and deep-breathing exercises. Aromatherapy allows us to learn which natural scents can calm our spirits. Visualization techniques can cause us to feel as if we are transported to a calmer time and place. If we can learn to embrace these relaxation tools as a society, we can reverse the stress that plagues us.

Tyler Harris

Columbus, Ohio

? Questions

1   The author contrasts the way people acted in the past with the way people act today to show that

   A. people in the past took more vacations.

   B. the past was better than the present.

   C. society has changed a lot over time.

   D. people today work too hard.

 Read the passage again. What has contributed to the way people act today as opposed to the way they acted in the past?

2   Which statement reflects the author's views about today's society?

   A. People need to start spending more time with their families.

   B. Exercise is a great way to both get in shape and relax.

   C. Men and women should choose between staying home and going to work.

   D. It is important that people take time to relieve the stress in their lives.

 Skim the article again and think about the main idea. Then try to eliminate incorrect answer choices. Also, try to determine the author's main purpose for writing the letter.

3   What is the focus of the passage?

   A. working too hard

   B. taking time to relax

   C. using new technologies

   D. remembering the past

 Several of the answer choices focus on details from the passage. Which one best describes the main idea presented in the passage?

Passage 2

Read the following passage. Then answer the questions that follow. Use the Tip below each question to help you choose the correct answer. When you finish, read the answer explanations at the end of this chapter.

Tarantula Tamer

by Jacqueline Ray

1   If you ask Sidney Reich about her work, she will say her job is the greatest in the world—although most people would disagree. Sidney is a scientist specializing in the study and protection of the tarantula, a hairy creature that makes most people cringe.

2   Reich says her fascination with insects, particularly arachnids (insects with an exoskeleton), began when she was just a little girl.

3   "I spent my early childhood in a rural town in Pennsylvania, where there weren't many children to play with. To occupy my time, I roamed the woods near my home, carefully studying every daddy longlegs and tick I could find. I quickly observed that different types of spiders spun different types of webs, and I could seek out a spider simply by spotting its web. When I was about twelve, my family moved to California, and I attended a much larger school. There I met many other kids who were interested in learning all about arachnids."

4   Reich said she first saw a tarantula when hiking with a friend.

5   "I could not believe my eyes! It was monstrous—a good three or four inches long—and the most incredible arthropod I had ever seen."

6   Reich explained that the tarantula did not reciprocate her interest and quickly scooted back into its burrow, but this didn't matter; she was already hooked and wanted to learn as much about tarantulas as possible.

7   Today Reich studies tarantulas in rainforests throughout the world. Since tarantulas are nocturnal, Reich observes them at night when they are active. When asked if her work is dangerous, Reich confesses that she has had a few close calls, but not with tarantulas. She has suffered several snakebites and even a scorpion bite. But Reich considers her suffering worthwhile if her research helps save tarantulas, some species of which are in danger of extinction. She explains that when most people see a tarantula, they are so frightened that they step on it and kill it on the spot.

8   "People don't realize that there is no record of a human ever dying from a tarantula bite and that most tarantulas hide from people rather than attack them."

9   Reich blames horror movies for the tarantula's reputation as aggressive and deadly. The destruction of the rainforests is another factor affecting the tarantula population.

10   "The more people learn about tarantulas, the better off the spiders will be," Reich concludes. "People will begin to appreciate tarantulas as an important part of nature and will not want to harm them."

⍰ Questions

4   Which sentence is a detail from the passage intended to convey that tarantulas are not nearly as harmful as people believe them to be?

A. The more people learn about tarantulas, the better off the spiders will be.

B. Reich said she first saw a tarantula when hiking with a friend.

C. Today Reich studies tarantulas in the rainforests throughout the world.

D. Reich blames horror movies for the tarantula's reputation as aggressive and deadly.

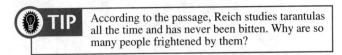

TIP According to the passage, Reich studies tarantulas all the time and has never been bitten. Why are so many people frightened by them?

5   What is the intended effect of the description of Reich given in this excerpt: "But Reich considers her suffering worthwhile if her research helps save tarantulas"? (paragraph 7)

   A. to show Reich's adventurous spirit

   B. to show how Reich became interested in tarantulas

   C. to show Reich's dedication to her work

   D. to show that Reich wanted to have an exciting career

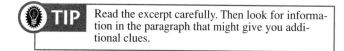

Read the excerpt carefully. Then look for information in the paragraph that might give you additional clues.

6   Why does the passage open with the line "If you ask Sidney Reich about her work, she will say her job is the greatest in the world—although most people would disagree"?

   A. to emphasize that Reich's job is anything but traditional

   B. to emphasize that Reich's job is incredibly dangerous

   C. to emphasize that Reich is defensive of her line of work

   D. to emphasize that Reich is proud of her accomplishments

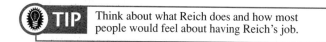

Think about what Reich does and how most people would feel about having Reich's job.

Passage 3

Read the following passage. Then answer the questions that follow. Use the Tip below each question to help you choose the correct answer. When you finish, read the answer explanations at the end of this chapter.

Don't Sweat Global Warming

Calvin Marks, the president of Marks Manufacturing Company, gave this speech at a recent convention to raise awareness about environmental laws that could create difficult challenges for many manufacturers and factories and have devastating effects on economies worldwide.

1   Good evening, ladies and gentlemen, and welcome.

2   I'm going to speak to you tonight about a topic that you've probably seen in the news quite a bit in the past few years: global warming. Recently, scientists have suggested that Earth is experiencing its warmest temperatures in more than a thousand years. This is fascinating and important news, but it has many people concerned. Some of these people view "global warming" as a major problem and want emergency laws to be passed to help reduce it. However, I believe that these people's concerns are unnecessary. Passing new global warming laws would do more harm than good to our world.

3   For several decades, scientists and concerned citizens have been exploring a theory called the "greenhouse effect." This theory holds that the warming of the planet is caused by human activity. Factories, automobiles and certain household appliances cause harmful gases to drift into the sky. Some of these pollutants are called "greenhouse gases." They are believed to gather in the atmosphere and trap heat. Acting like a giant greenhouse, these gases cause the earth to grow warmer.

4   Believing greenhouse gases to be a main cause of global warming, many companies and countries joined together to reduce the amount of greenhouse gases they can legally emit. However, since then, leaders all over the world have begun to question the wisdom of this decision. The laws they passed create a burden on companies worldwide and are not having a clear effect on global warming anyway.

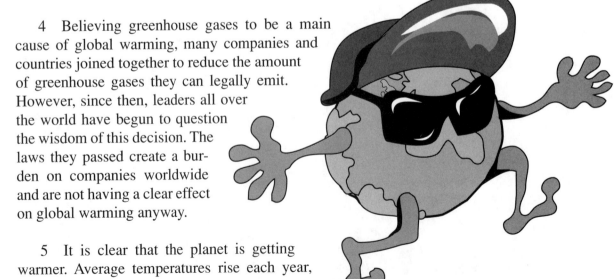

5   It is clear that the planet is getting warmer. Average temperatures rise each year,

and instances of record-breaking heat are more and more common. Also, there have been many unusual occurrences in the weather that may be tied to this warming, such as floods, droughts and storms.

6   What is not clear is that human beings are the cause of this warming. I feel that greenhouse gases and other air pollution, while being dangerous and harmful to our planet, are not the cause of global warming. In fact, global warming is probably caused by Earth itself. Throughout the history of the world, temperatures have changed, sometimes significantly. There were times of blistering heat, as well as freezing ice ages, long before humans even existed. There was even a "mini Ice Age" as recently as a few hundred years ago. Earth's temperature simply changes for reasons that are far beyond people's control.

7   People who still believe that greenhouse gases cause global warming have been pushing for new laws to reduce the gases. These laws would be aimed at changing the fuels we use and regulating, or even shutting down, businesses that emit greenhouse gases.

8   If these laws were passed, it would be a disaster for our economy. The laws would force many important businesses to stop production while they removed greenhouse gases from their factories. This "cleanup" might take weeks or months, during which time the companies could lose millions of dollars. Meanwhile, consumers would be deprived of the companies' products.

9   Additionally, the effect of such laws on many foreign economies could be downright devastating. The United States has many computer-based technological businesses that would not be altered by the laws. However, many other nations, especially developing ones, rely on factories. If their factories were shut down, these countries would lose an essential part of their economy and society. This would be tragic, especially since most greenhouse gases are produced by the United States and other, wealthier nations. Less fortunate countries would be made to suffer for the mistakes and misdeeds of Americans. Is that fair?

10   Even if these laws were put into effect and the world economy survived them, there is no guarantee that the laws would yield any positive results. Let's say that alternative sources of fuel and energy that do not produce greenhouse gases are put into widespread use. Who can say if these fuels will be effective? Also, almost every kind of fuel will have some harmful byproduct. Just because one type of energy leaves behind no greenhouse gases does not mean it is safe for the environment. For instance, nuclear power leaves behind poisonous nuclear wastes; even the so-called cleanest energies, solar and wind power, require the deforestation of large amounts of land. No kind of power is perfect, and the fuels that cause greenhouse gases are by no means the worst.

11   Despite these many reasonable objections to anti–greenhouse gas laws, many people continue to push for them. These people insist that greenhouse gases cause global warming and that global warming will culminate in global disaster. This idea has no foundation at all. As mentioned earlier, the temperature on Earth rises and falls naturally. There are cold periods and warm periods that occur randomly and without any sort of human interference. Global warming is natural and will not destroy the planet or its inhabitants.

12   People are continually overestimating the possible dangers of global warming and the effects of greenhouse gases. They claim that the heating of the planet may cause diseases like malaria to spread, kill vegetation and the animals that rely on it, encourage wildfires and melt the polar ice caps. The final point is considered the most dangerous. If the polar ice caps melted, more water would be added to the oceans, causing them to rise. This can cause massive, deadly floods and would have the potential to permanently cover entire countries with water. These claims sound compelling, but they are not realistic.

13   The situation is not nearly as bad as many people insist. As scientists learn more and more about the warming of our planet, they continually realize that the effects of the warming will not be so dangerous. Only minute changes will take place, even over the course of many hundreds of years. There will be no sudden catastrophes because of global warming.

14   Earth is indeed warming, but it is a slow and entirely natural process. Global warming will not lead to disasters, and it is not caused by anything humans are doing or failing to do. People can pass thousands of laws to regulate factories, cars and any other human-made objects, but this will have no effect on global warming. These laws will only make life harder for the people of Earth.

(?) Questions

7   Give two reasons why people want to pass new laws concerning the emission of greenhouse gases, and contrast them with two reasons why creating more regulations would be harmful. Write your answer on the lines below.

_____

_____

_____

_____

 TIP   Skim the passage for details that will support your answer.

8   Which statement reflects the author's views about global warming?

    A. Global warming is an unnatural result of pollution.

    B. Global warming may cause diseases in humans.

    C. Global warming is not as serious as people think.

    D. Global warming should be controlled by legislation.

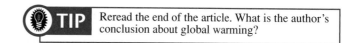

TIP Reread the end of the article. What is the author's conclusion about global warming?

9   What is the intended effect of the rhetorical question used in paragraph 9?

    A. to serve as a topic sentence

    B. to stimulate reader interest

    C. to produce an echoing sound when read aloud

    D. to create patterns of stressed and unstressed syllables

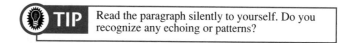

TIP Read the paragraph silently to yourself. Do you recognize any echoing or patterns?

10   The phrase "will culminate in global disaster" (paragraph 11) is used to describe the belief that

    A. global disaster can be easily prevented.

    B. global warming will lead to global disaster.

    C. global disaster has already occurred.

    D. global warming is the same as global disaster.

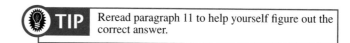

TIP Reread paragraph 11 to help yourself figure out the correct answer.

Passage 4

Read the following passage. Then answer the questions that follow. Use the Tip below each question to help you choose the correct answer. When you finish, read the answer explanations at the end of this chapter.

The Truth About Year-Round Education
by Rebecca Simonson

No More Teachers, No More Books . . .

1   Summer. For many students, it means a vacation with their families, time to relax with their friends or an opportunity to make some extra money at a summer job. But believe it or not, summer still means school for some students. These kids aren't attending classes because of poor grades or to try to get ahead but because their school districts run on the innovative year-round schedule.

2   The traditional ten-month school schedule that most students are accustomed to was formed at a time when many Americans lived on farms. In the summer, children were needed to help their families work the fields and prepare for the fall harvest. Even after farming declined, many schools stuck with the original schedule because many felt that it was too hot to keep students cooped up inside all day during a time when many schools lacked air-conditioning systems. However, in recent years, there has been a movement to institute year-round education in school districts throughout the United States.

How Year-Round Education Really Works

3   Despite what many people think, many students who go to school year-round don't spend more days in class than children who attend traditional schools. Unlike the extended-school-year program, which considerably lengthens the time that children spend in school, most year-round programs require students to spend the traditional 170 to 180 days in class, but vacation time is broken up throughout the year.

4   Some schools use a single-track system. This means that all students and faculty are in session and take breaks at the same time. This system has several subsystems that include a flexible all-year calendar that allows students and teachers to take short breaks when it is convenient for them. Modified schedules are also used in this system. Some schools will have forty-five days of instruction followed by a fifteen-day break, while others keep students and teachers in class for ninety days and then break for thirty days.

5   Multitrack systems are also used in year-round education, usually by schools that have overcrowding issues. Multitrack systems usually have three to five tracks, and each

student is assigned to a specific track. While students in certain tracks are in school, one or two other tracks will be on vacation. This is generally used so that a school can house more students without having to build new schools or shipping students to other districts.

Benefits

6   Besides allowing school districts to accommodate an ever-growing number of students, year-round education is thought to have many more benefits. Some argue that cutting out the long summer break decreases the amount of information students lose while not receiving instruction. This allows teachers to focus more on new material rather than wasting time reviewing at the beginning of the year.

7   Others feel that more frequent breaks mean that both students and teachers will be absent less often because this schedule allows for time to rest and relax during the school year. Another appealing aspect to the unorthodox system is that the program not only helps to alleviate overcrowding but may also save taxpayers money that would need to be spent creating new schools and hiring faculty. Supporters of the system also argue that year-round education is used throughout the world in many countries where students perform better academically than their U.S. counterparts.

Drawbacks

8   Of course, there are those that believe that a year-round school system is not the answer to America's educational problems. Critics argue that doing away with summer vacation will greatly disrupt many families' social schedules. Parents of young children will have to find someone to watch their kids during the short breaks because the camps and special activities usually offered during the summer months are not available. Also, many feel that extracurricular activities would suffer under the year-round education system. Sports and music events often require interactions between school districts. If one school is year-round and the other is not, scheduling a time for such activities could be very difficult.

9   The most important argument against the system is that there is no statistically significant evidence showing that year-round education improves students' academic abilities or increases standardized test scores. Supporters argue that this is not the case, but critics point to several studies that show only minor improvements in students participating in year-round education.

So Long, Summer?

10   According to the National Association for Year-Round Education, 3,045 American schools had adopted this alternative educational system by the 2005-2006 school year, including seven school districts in Ohio. Does this mean that students should live in fear of the day when their summers are no longer their own? Well, let's just say they shouldn't throw in their beach towels just yet.

11 Parents, teachers and students across the United States continue to debate the positive and negative aspects of the program. The topic remains a controversial one, and many school districts have opposed a switch. But the truth is, American students continue to lag behind children in Europe and Asia academically. Perhaps a little less fun in the sun and a little more time in the classroom might be just what students need to help them get ahead.

(?) Questions

11 The author says a year-round school schedule

  A. shows no evidence of being better than a traditional schedule.

  B. can provide students with a better education.

  C. benefits families by giving them more vacation time to spend together.

  D. helps students improve their grades and test scores.

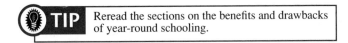

TIP Reread the sections on the benefits and drawbacks of year-round schooling.

12 The phrase "throw in their beach towels" (paragraph 10) is used to mean

  A. give up hope.

  B. change their minds.

  C. make vacation plans.

  D. voice their support.

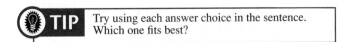

TIP Try using each answer choice in the sentence. Which one fits best?

13 Which is a detail from the passage intended to convey that the traditional ten-month school schedule is outdated and no longer necessary?

  A. Schools need to rotate schedules to accommodate more students.

  B. European and Asian children are further ahead in school than American children.

  C. Farmers needed their children at home in the summer to help work in the fields.

  D. Teachers must review old material to refresh students' memories after a break.

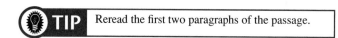

TIP | Reread the first two paragraphs of the passage.

14 Based on paragraph 11, which would the author support?

  A. extended breaks following each quarter of the school year

  B. instituting a year-round school schedule at her child's school

  C. educating people about the drawbacks of year-round schooling

  D. temporarily enrolling her child in a different school district

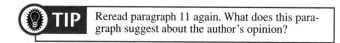

TIP | Reread paragraph 11 again. What does this paragraph suggest about the author's opinion?

Answers and Explanations

1 C

The author uses examples from the past in his letter to show the reader how much our society has changed. His explanations show readers that while some of the advances in our society have made our lives easier, they can also contribute to the amount of stress in people's lives.

2 D

The author never says that people should spend more time with their families, just that they need to take more time to relax. The author recommends several relaxation techniques, not just exercise. Also, while the author says that in the past men and women fulfilled separate roles, he never suggests that they choose between home and work. Answer choice D is correct.

3 B

The discussions of people working too hard, using new technologies and remembering how things were in the past are all details in the passage. Only answer choice B explains what the entire passage is about: taking the time to relax.

4 D

According to Reich, there is no record of a person's ever having died from a tarantula bite. The article goes on to say that tarantulas' portrayal in movies as a deadly spider has scared many people.

5 C

The author specifically mentions Reich's research in this sentence, which shows that Reich is truly dedicated to her work even though it can be dangerous.

6 A

From reading the passage, you can tell that Reich is proud of her work and that her job is sometimes dangerous. She would also be the first to tell you that tarantulas are not as bad as people think. However, the main reason the author begins the passage with this sentence is to show that Reich's job is not the average job.

7 Sample answer

Some people want new laws to regulate greenhouse gas emissions because they believe that greenhouse gases produced by factories and automobiles trap heat and are causing global warming. They think that regulating emissions will help to stop global warming. Another reason people want these laws is that they think that greenhouse gases will eventually trap so much heat that the polar ice caps will melt and Earth's oceans will rise, engulfing entire countries. According to the passage, however, creating more laws concerning greenhouse gases will put more strain on factories and automobile makers, which will weaken economies all over the world. Additionally, the speaker points out that even cleaner forms of energy, such as nuclear energy, leave behind harmful toxins. Moreover, other forms of energy, such as solar power or wind power, require large sections of land to be cleared for use.

8 C

The author clearly indicates that people are too concerned with global warming and that it is not as serious as people think.

9 B

The purpose of the rhetorical question is to stimulate readers' interest. The question offers no echoing sound or pattern of syllables. Also, the topic sentence of the paragraph is the first sentence, not the last sentence.

10 B

Culminate means "to conclude or end." In this statement, the narrator is saying that some people believe that global warming will lead to a global disaster.

11 A

According to the passage, there is no "statistically significant evidence" to suggest that year-round schooling is better than traditional schooling. Answer choice A is correct.

12 A

The phrase "throw in the towel" means "to give up on something." Here the author says "throw in their beach towels" because she is discussing the possibility of students' giving up hope of having long summer vacations.

13 C

According to the passage, the traditional ten-month school schedule was put in place because farmers needed their children to help work the fields in the summer. Also, many felt it was too hot in the summer to keep kids inside.

14 B

In paragraph 11, the author points out that American children lag behind European and Asian children in school, and that spending more time in the classroom might help American students achieve better grades. Answer choice B is correct.

Chapter 6

Literary Texts

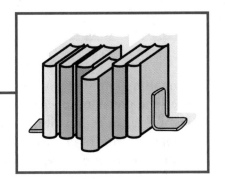

Benchmarks

Reading Applications: Literary Text

A. Analyze interactions between characters in literary text and how the interactions affect the plot.

C. Identify the structural elements of the plot and explain how an author develops conflicts and plot to pace the events in literary text.

Grade Level Indicators

1. Compare and contrast an author's use of direct and indirect characterization, and ways in which characters reveal traits about themselves, including dialect, dramatic monologues and soliloquies.

3. Distinguish how conflicts, parallel plots and subplots affect the pacing of action in literary text.

7. Explain how literary techniques, including foreshadowing and flashback, are used to shape plot of a literary text.

8. Recognize how irony is used in a literary text.

Literary Elements

Questions on the OGT for this standard will be on fiction or literary passages. The passages may be excerpts from short stories, memoirs, poems, novels or plays. The questions will ask about literary elements such as irony. This section of the test will contain multiple-choice, short-response and extended-response questions.

Conflict and Resolution

Typically, a short story revolves around a conflict, which is a major problem that the characters must face. Some questions on the OGT will ask you to identify story conflicts. Others will ask you how characters resolve conflicts, or reach resolutions.

Characterization

Questions for this standard will also be about characterization. Often these questions will ask you why a character behaved a certain way. They also might ask you which sentence illustrates a specific trait of a certain character.

Passage 1

Read the following passage. Then answer the questions that follow. Use the Tip below each question to help you choose the correct answer. When you finish, read the answer explanations at the end of this chapter.

Ah, Are You Digging on My Grave?
by Thomas Hardy

1 "Ah, are you digging on my grave,

    My loved one?—planting rue?"

    —"No: yesterday he went to wed

    One of the brightest wealth has bred.

    'It cannot hurt her now,' he said,

    'That I should not be true.'"

2 "Then who is digging on my grave,

    My nearest dearest kin?"

    —"Ah, no: they sit and think, 'What use!

    What good will planting flowers produce?

    No tendance of her mound can loose

    Her spirit from Death's gin.'"

3 "But someone digs upon my grave?

    My enemy?—prodding sly?"

    —"Nay: when she heard you had passed the Gate

    That shuts on all flesh soon or late,

    She thought you no more worth her hate,

    And cares not where you lie."

4 "Then, who is digging on my grave?

Say—since I have not guessed!"

—"O it is I, my mistress dear,

Your little dog, who still lives near,

And much I hope my movements here

Have not disturbed your rest?"

5 "Ah yes! You dig upon my grave . . .

Why flashed it not to me

That one true heart was left behind!

What feeling do we ever find

To equal among human kind

A dog's fidelity!"

6 "Mistress, I dug upon your grave

To bury a bone, in case

I should be hungry near this spot

When passing on my daily trot.

I am sorry, but I quite forgot

It was your resting place."

❓ Questions

1. Why was the dog digging on the grave?

    A. It got hungry on its walk.

    B. It heard its owner talking.

    C. It was hiding its bone.

    D. It wanted to see its owner.

 TIP   Read the end of the poem carefully.

2 Explain how the speaker's characterization of herself helps to express the main idea of the poem. Give three examples or pieces of information from the story to support your explanation.

_____

_____

_____

_____

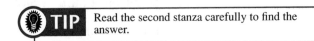

TIP From reading the poem, what do you know about the speaker? What does she want?

3 What accounts for the family's failure to plant flowers on the speaker's grave?

A. thinking that she would not like flowers

B. unwillingness to admit she has passed

C. worry that the dog would destroy them

D. knowing that the flowers will not bring her back

TIP Read the second stanza carefully to find the answer.

Passage 2

Read the following passage. Then answer the questions that follow. Use the Tip below each question to help you choose the correct answer. When you finish, read the answer explanations at the end of this chapter.

Ripe Figs
by Kate Chopin

1   Maman-Nainaine said that when the figs were ripe Babette might go to visit her cousins down on Bayou-Boeuf, where the sugar cane grows. Not that the ripening of figs had the least thing to do with it, but that is the way Maman-Nainaine was.

2   It seemed to Babette a very long time to wait; for the leaves upon the trees were tender yet, and the figs were like little hard, green marbles.

3   But warm rains came along and plenty of strong sunshine; and though Maman-Nainaine was as patient as the statue of la Madone, and Babette as restless as a humming-bird, the first thing they both knew it was hot summer-time. Every day Babette danced out to where the fig-trees were in a long line against the fence. She walked slowly beneath them, carefully peering between the gnarled, spreading branches. But each time she came disconsolate away again. What she saw there finally was something that made her sing and dance the whole day long.

4   When Maman-Nainaine sat down in her stately way to breakfast, the following morning, her muslin cap standing like an aureole about her white, placid face, Babette approached. She bore a dainty porcelain platter, which she set down before her godmother. It contained a dozen purple figs, fringed around with their rich, green leaves.

5   "Ah," said Maman-Nainaine, arching her eyebrows, "how early the figs have ripened this year!"

6   "Oh," said Babette, "I think they have ripened very late."

7   "Babette," continued Maman-Nainaine, as she peeled the very plumpest figs with her pointed silver fruit-knife, "you will carry my love to them all down on Bayou-Boeuf. And tell your tante Frosine I shall look for her at Toussaint—when the chrysanthemums are in bloom."

(?) Questions

4   Which sentence explains the lesson Maman-Nainaine wants to teach Babette?

   A. We appreciate things more if we wait for them.

   B. Figs take an awfully long time to become ripe.

   C. Looking forward to something is entertaining.

   D. It is important to learn to have patience.

 TIP Remember that Maman-Nainaine thinks the figs have ripened early and Babette thinks they have ripened very late. Which detail in this story is the most important lesson?

5   Why does Maman-Nainaine tell Babette to wait until the figs ripen?

   A. She wants Babette to ignore her own family.

   B. She does not approve of Babette having fun.

   C. She does not want Babette to travel until summer.

   D. She wants Babette to serve the ripened figs to her.

 TIP Read through the story and think about the details the author gives. Of the choices that are offered, to which do the details seem to point?

6   The significant difference between Maman-Nainaine and Babette is that

   A. Maman-Nainaine is mean and Babette is friendly.

   B. Maman-Nainaine is unruffled and Babette is anxious.

   C. Maman-Nainaine acts selfishly and Babette does not.

   D. Maman-Nainaine likes figs and Babette does not.

 TIP Pay close attention to what is being suggested in these choices. Which choice is backed by evidence in the text?

Passage 3

Read the following passage. Then answer the questions that follow. Use the Tip below each question to help you choose the correct answer. When you finish, read the answer explanations at the end of this chapter.

Excerpt from *Hamlet*
by William Shakespeare

Hamlet's father, the King of Denmark, has recently died. Shortly after the king's death, Hamlet's mother married Hamlet's uncle, Claudius, who is the new king. After hearing from his friends that a ghost resembling his father has been sighted wandering around the castle, Hamlet has agreed to stand watch with them at the castle gates in hopes of seeing his father's figure appear.

1   **Scene IV. The platform.**

[*Enter Hamlet, Horatio, and Marcellus.*]

HAMLET: The air bites shrewdly; it is very cold.

HORATIO: It is a nipping and an eager air.

5   HAMLET: What hour now?

HORATIO: I think it lacks of twelve.

MARCELLUS: No, it is struck.

HORATIO: Indeed? I heard it not: then draws near the season

Wherein the spirit held his wont to walk. . . .

10   Look, my lord, it comes!

[*Enter Ghost.*]

HAMLET: Angels and ministers of grace defend us!—

Be thou a spirit of health or goblin damn'd,

Bring with thee airs from heaven or blasts from hell,

15   Be thy intents wicked or charitable,

Thou com'st in such a questionable shape

That I will speak to thee: I'll call thee Hamlet,

King, father, royal Dane; O, answer me!

Let me not burst in ignorance; but tell

20 Why thy canoniz'd bones, hearsed in death,

Have burst their cerements; why the sepulchre,

Wherein we saw thee quietly in-urn'd,

Hath op'd his ponderous and marble jaws

To cast thee up again! What may this mean,

25 That thou, dead corse, again in complete steel,

Revisit'st thus the glimpses of the moon,

Making night hideous, and we fools of nature

So horridly to shake our disposition

With thoughts beyond the reaches of our souls?

30 Say, why is this? wherefore? what should we do?

[*Ghost beckons Hamlet.*]

HORATIO: It beckons you to go away with it,

As if it some impartment did desire

To you alone.

35 MARCELLUS: Look with what courteous action

It waves you to a more removed ground:

But do not go with it!

HORATIO: No, by no means.

HAMLET: It will not speak; then will I follow it.

40 HORATIO: Do not, my lord.

HAMLET: Why, what should be the fear?

I do not set my life at a pin's fee;

And for my soul, what can it do to that,

Being a thing immortal as itself?

45 It waves me forth again;—I'll follow it.

HORATIO: What if it tempt you toward the flood, my lord,

Or to the dreadful summit of the cliff

That beetles o'er his base into the sea,

And there assume some other horrible form

50   Which might deprive your sovereignty of reason,

And draw you into madness? think of it:

The very place puts toys of desperation,

Without more motive, into every brain

That looks so many fadoms to the sea

55   And hears it roar beneath.

HAMLET: It waves me still.—

Go on; I'll follow thee.

MARCELLUS: You shall not go, my lord.

HAMLET: Hold off your hands.

60   HORATIO: Be rul'd; you shall not go.

HAMLET: My fate cries out,

And makes each petty artery in this body

As hardy as the Nemean lion's nerve.—

[*Ghost beckons.*]

65   Still am I call'd;—unhand me, gentlemen;—

[*Breaking free from them.*]

By heaven, I'll make a ghost of him that lets me!—

I say, away!—Go on; I'll follow thee.

[*Exeunt Ghost and Hamlet.*]

70   HORATIO: He waxes desperate with imagination.

MARCELLUS: Let's follow; 'tis not fit thus to obey him.

HORATIO: Have after.—To what issue will this come?

MARCELLUS: Something is rotten in the state of Denmark.

HORATIO: Heaven will direct it.

75   MARCELLUS: Nay, let's follow him.

[*Exeunt.*]

Scene V. A more remote part of the Castle.

[Enter Ghost and Hamlet.]

HAMLET: Whither wilt thou lead me? speak! I'll go no further.

80   GHOST: Mark me.

HAMLET: I will.

GHOST: My hour is almost come,

When I to sulph'uous and tormenting flames

Must render up myself.

85   HAMLET: Alas, poor ghost!

GHOST: Pity me not, but lend thy serious hearing

To what I shall unfold.

HAMLET: Speak; I am bound to hear.

GHOST: So art thou to revenge, when thou shalt hear.

90   HAMLET: What?

GHOST: I am thy father's spirit;

Doom'd for a certain term to walk the night,

And for the day confin'd to fast in fires,

Till the foul crimes done in my days of nature

95   Are burnt and purg'd away. But that I am forbid

To tell the secrets of my prison-house,

I could a tale unfold whose lightest word

Would harrow up thy soul; freeze thy young blood;

Make thy two eyes, like stars, start from their spheres;

100   Thy knotted and combined locks to part,

And each particular hair to stand on end

Like quills upon the fretful porcupine:

But this eternal blazon must not be

To ears of flesh and blood.—List, list, O, list!—

105   If thou didst ever thy dear father love— . . .

Revenge his foul and most unnatural murder.

HAMLET: Murder!

GHOST: Murder most foul, as in the best it is;

But this most foul, strange, and unnatural.

110   HAMLET: Haste me to know't, that I, with wings as swift

As meditation or the thoughts of love,

May sweep to my revenge.

GHOST: I find thee apt;

And duller shouldst thou be than the fat weed

115   That rots itself in ease on Lethe wharf,

Wouldst thou not stir in this. Now, Hamlet, hear.

'Tis given out that, sleeping in my orchard,

A serpent stung me; so the whole ear of Denmark

Is by a forged process of my death

120   Rankly abus'd; but know, thou noble youth,

The serpent that did sting thy father's life

Now wears his crown.

HAMLET: O my prophetic soul!

Mine uncle!

? Questions

7   What accounts for Horatio's and Marcellus's reluctance to let Hamlet go with the ghost?

A. fear that the ghost will hurt Hamlet

B. worry that Claudius will find out

C. thinking that the ghost is a trick

D. concern that Hamlet will never return

TIP   Reread the conversation between Horatio and Hamlet.

8   Which sentence explains the actual cause of Hamlet's father's death?

   A. He was killed by Hamlet's uncle.

   B. He was bitten by a poisonous snake.

   C. He passed away in his sleep.

   D. He got trapped in a raging fire.

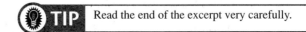

TIP   Read the end of the excerpt very carefully.

9   Why does the ghost want to talk to Hamlet?

   A. He wants to tell Hamlet not to pity him.

   B. He wants to keep Hamlet from the flames.

   C. He wants to warn Hamlet of the future.

   D. He wants to tell Hamlet how he died.

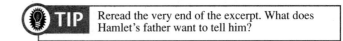

TIP   Reread the very end of the excerpt. What does Hamlet's father want to tell him?

10   Why can't the ghost tell Hamlet what happened at the prison-house?

   A. The ghost would burn in the flames.

   B. The ghost is forbidden to discuss it.

   C. Hamlet would seek revenge.

   D. Others might overhear the ghost.

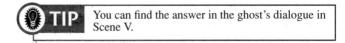

TIP   You can find the answer in the ghost's dialogue in Scene V.

Passage 4

Read the following passage. Then answer the questions that follow. Use the Tip below each question to help you choose the correct answer. When you finish, read the answer explanations at the end of this chapter.

Excerpt from "The Hypnotist"
by Ambrose Bierce

1   My first knowledge that I possessed unusual powers came to me in my fourteenth year, when at school. Happening one day to have forgotten to bring my noon-day luncheon, I gazed longingly at that of a small girl who was preparing to eat hers. Looking up, her eyes met mine and she seemed unable to withdraw them. After a moment of hesitancy she came forward in an absent kind of way and without a word surrendered her little basket with its tempting contents and walked away. Inexpressibly pleased, I relieved my hunger and destroyed the basket. After that I had not the trouble to bring a luncheon for myself: that little girl was my daily purveyor. . . . The girl was always persuaded that she had eaten all herself; and later in the day her tearful complaints of hunger surprised the teacher, entertained the pupils, earned for her the sobriquet of Greedy-Gut and filled me with a peace past understanding. . . .

2   For some years afterward I had little opportunity to practice hypnotism; such small essays as I made at it were commonly barren of other recognition than solitary confinement on a bread-and-water diet; sometimes, indeed, they elicited nothing better than the cat-o'-nine-tails. It was when I was about to leave the scene of these small disappointments that my one really important feat was performed.

3   I had been called into the warden's office and given a suit of civilian's clothing, a trifling sum of money and a great deal of advice, which I am bound to confess was of a much better quality than the clothing. As I was passing out of the gate into the light of freedom I suddenly turned and looking the warden gravely in the eye, soon had him in control.

4   "You are an ostrich," I said.

5   At the post-mortem examination the stomach was found to contain a great quantity of indigestible articles mostly of wood or metal. Stuck fast in the esophagus and constituting, according to the Coroner's jury, the immediate cause of death, one door-knob.

6   I was by nature a good and affectionate son, but as I took my way into the great world from which I had been so long secluded I could not help remembering that all my misfortunes had flowed like a stream from . . . my parents in the matter of school luncheons; and I knew of no reason to think they had reformed. . . .

7   It was while going afoot to South Asphyxia, the home of my childhood, that I found both my parents on their way to the Hill. They had hitched their team and were eating lun-

cheon under an oak tree in the center of the field. The sight of the luncheon called up painful memories of my school days and roused the sleeping lion in my breast.

8   Approaching the guilty couple, who at once recognized me, I ventured to suggest that I share their hospitality.

9   "Of this cheer, my son," said the author of my being, with characteristic pomposity, which age had not withered, "there is sufficient for but two. I am not, I hope, insensible to the hunger-light in your eyes, but—"

10   My father has never completed that sentence; what he mistook for hunger-light was simply the earnest gaze of the hypnotist. In a few seconds he was at my service. A few more sufficed for the lady, and the dictates of a just resentment could be carried into effect. "My former father," I said, "I presume that it is known to you that you and this lady are no longer what you were?"

11   "I have observed a certain subtle change," was the rather dubious reply of the old gentleman; "it is perhaps attributable to age."

12   "It is more than that," I explained; "it goes to character—to species. You and the lady here are, in truth, two broncos—wild stallions both, and unfriendly."

13   "Why, John," exclaimed my dear mother, "you don't mean to say that I am—"

14   "Madam," I replied, solemnly, fixing my eyes again upon hers, "you are."

15   Scarcely had the words fallen from my lips when she dropped upon her hands and knees, and backing up to the old man squealed like a demon and delivered a vicious kick upon his shin! An instant later he was himself down on all-fours, headed away from her and flinging his feet. . . . With equal earnestness but inferior agility, because of her hampering body-gear, she plied her own. Their flying legs crossed and mingled in the most bewildering way. . . . On recovering themselves they would resume the combat, uttering their frenzy in the nameless sounds of the furious brutes which they believed themselves to be—the whole region rang with their clamor! . . . Wild, inarticulate screams of rage attested the delivery of the blows; groans, grunts and gasps their receipt. Nothing more truly military was ever seen at Gettysburg or Waterloo: the valor of my dear parents in the hour of danger can never cease to be to me a source of pride and gratification. . . .

16   Arrested for provoking a breach of the peace, I was, and have ever since been, tried in the Court of Technicalities and Continuances whence, after fifteen years of proceedings, my attorney is moving heaven and earth to get the case taken to the Court of Remandment for New Trials.

17   Such are a few of my principal experiments in the mysterious force or agency known as hypnotic suggestion. Whether or not it could be employed by a bad man for an unworthy purpose I am unable to say.

 **Questions**

11 Identify two examples of how irony is used in the story. Write your answer in the space provided.

_____

_____

_____

_____

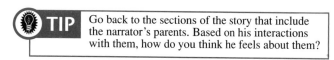

| **TIP** | Look for places in the story where ideas or actions seem to have double meanings. |

12 Which statement characterizes the narrator's feelings toward his parents?

A. He forgives them for most of their mistakes.

B. He is mad at them for not being generous.

C. He thinks they did an okay job raising him.

D. He feels that they are incredibly virtuous.

| **TIP** | Go back to the sections of the story that include the narrator's parents. Based on his interactions with them, how do you think he feels about them? |

13 What accounts for the narrator's doubt about whether his powers can be used for an "unworthy purpose"?

    A. dissatisfaction with his powers

    B. doubting his parents' sincerity

    C. the success of his experiment

    D. thinking his actions are not bad

 Eliminate answer choices that are obviously incorrect. Then think about the last statement in the story. How does it affect your understanding of the story?

14 Why did the school children call the little girl at the beginning of the story Greedy-Gut?

    A. She always ate other people's lunches.

    B. She was still hungry after lunchtime.

    C. She always finished her lunch first.

    D. She was never happy with her lunch.

 Reread the beginning of the story carefully.

Answers and Explanations

1   C

The dog digs on the grave because he wants to hide a dog bone there.

2   **Sample answer**

The main idea of this poem is that while we wonder who is paying attention to us and what others think of us, most of the world is indifferent to our interior thoughts. The speaker characterizes herself as someone who wants some attention, someone who wants to be loved and remembered, not unlike most people. However, the poem shows readers that the world is more indifferent to these desires than we would like to believe.

The speaker progresses from questioning the person who should be closest to her to questioning her archenemy. First, her lover is too busy marrying for money to weep at her grave. Second, her family does not see the use in beautifying her grave, because it will not bring her back. Third, the speaker's enemy does not think much about the deceased. All these comments show that the world is indifferent to individuals. The speaker's repeated reaching out and asking "Who is on my grave?" helps to convey the main idea that though we spend a lot of time wondering what others think, others are mostly indifferent to these thoughts.

3   D

The speaker's family believes that putting flowers on her grave is a waste of time, because it will not bring her back to life.

4   D

The reason Maman-Nainaine makes Babette wait until the figs ripen is to teach her patience. Answer choice D is the correct answer.

5   C

The ripening of the figs coincides with the beginning of summer, according to the details revealed in the story. None of the other answer choices is backed up by evidence in the text. Answer choice C is correct.

6   B

The only assertion that is backed up by details in the text is that Maman-Nainaine is un-ruffled and Babette is anxious.

7   A

Horatio warns Hamlet that the ghost may tempt him toward a flood or the dreadful summit of the cliff. He and Marcellus fear the ghost will harm Hamlet.

8   A

In lines 117 through 122, the ghost of Hamlet's father explains that the people of Denmark were told that he was bitten by a snake. However, he tells Hamlet that the "snake" wears his crown, revealing that he was actually murder by Claudius, Hamlet's uncle.

9   D

Although the ghost does tell Hamlet not to pity him, he has come to see Hamlet to let him know that his uncle is a traitor who murdered him.

10   B

The ghost says he is forbidden to tell the tales of his prison-house.

11   **Sample answer**

The most obvious instance of irony in this story is in the last paragraph. The narrator says that he does not know whether his powers can be used for evil. This is ironic because he has been using his powers for evil throughout the story.

Another example of irony is when the narrator describes his parents' fight by saying "the valor of my dear parents in the hour of danger can never cease to be to me a source of pride and gratification." It is ironic that the narrator refers to their actions as valor, because their actions seem more comical or barbaric. It is also ironic that he takes pride in his parents at all, given the contempt he seems to feel toward them.

12   B

The author mentions in the middle of the story that he blames his parents' not having given him big enough lunches for the horrible things he does in his life. His later treatment of his parents when they will not share their picnic reiterates his anger at them.

13   D

The final statement by the narrator conveys how he has no remorse for his actions. He is not sure if the power can be used for unworthy causes because he does not consider his actions "unworthy."

14   B

According to the narrator, the little girl earned the nickname Greedy-Gut because after lunchtime she would cry that she was still hungry.

Chapter 7

Nonfiction Texts

Benchmarks

Reading Applications: Informational, Technical and Persuasive Text

A. Evaluate how features and characteristics make information accessible and usable and how structures help authors achieve their purposes.

C. Analyze whether graphics supplement textual information and promote the author's purpose.

Grade Level Indicators

1. Identify and understand organizational patterns (e.g., cause-effect, problem-solution) and techniques, including repetition of ideas, syntax and word choice, that authors use to accomplish their purposes and reach their intended audiences.

3. Evaluate the effectiveness of information found in maps, charts, tables, graphs, diagrams, cutaways and overlays.

7. Analyze the effectiveness of the features (e.g., format, graphics, sequence, headers) used in various consumer documents (e.g., warranties, product information, instructional materials), functional or workplace documents (e.g., job-related materials, memoranda, instructions) and public documents (e.g., speeches, newspaper editorials).

Reading and Understanding Nonfiction

In Chapter 6, you learned about the elements of fiction and literary texts. You can use that knowledge when reading novels, poetry, short stories or works of drama. However, a wide range of writings—such as letters, journals, essays, textbooks and reports—do not fit into the literary category. To understand these kinds of works, you need to know the elements of nonfiction.

Like fiction, nonfiction comes in various forms. The questions on the OGT may require you to analyze different types of nonfiction. These are some of the major purposes of nonfiction writing:

- **Informational:** written works that inform the reader of facts, figures and details

- **Technical:** documents, such as instruction manuals, that explain how to perform a certain action

- **Persuasive:** letters, speeches, essays or advertisements that try to convince readers to accept the author's point of view

Regardless of what type of nonfiction you are reading, you should get as much information as possible from it. To do this, you need to use all the materials the author provides for you. These may include maps, charts, tables, graphs and other graphics. The OGT will ask you to consider the reason an author might have chosen to add a particular graphic to his or her writing. You will need to decide what purpose the graphic serves or what other type of graphic might be more useful.

To understand nonfiction, you should also be aware of the other choices authors make. Authors must carefully choose how to arrange each piece of writing. An author might choose to employ several kinds of organization, such as chronological, cause and effect or problem and solution, to display the main points of the passage and make them meaningful to the reader.

Additionally, an author will likely make choices about the format and other features of the document. The OGT might ask you to decide why an author asks the reader a question or opens with a dramatic statement. You also might be asked why a passage is divided by headers or why information is organized into a list. To answer these types of questions, you will need to think about the author's purpose for writing. By determining what the point of the passage is, you will be better able to understand the many features of nonfiction.

Passage 1

Read the following passage. Then answer the questions that follow. Use the Tip below each question to help you choose the correct answer. When you finish, read the answer explanations at the end of this chapter.

Fuel of the Future
by Shelby Greene

1   Just because you don't see a biodiesel gas station on every street corner doesn't mean you cannot start incorporating this fuel into your life. With the cost of gas on the rise and politicians talking about a mandatory freeze on our use of fossil fuels, biodiesel is becoming a viable option for powering our vehicles. The government is generating all sorts of incentives to convince people to switch to biodiesel, including big tax breaks. Last year, U.S. production of biodiesel tripled. Politicians are getting behind biodiesel, or fuel partly manufactured from plants, because it solves two of our nation's biggest problems:

- Americans can begin to break their addiction to fossil fuels.

- The struggling business of agriculture will get a huge boost from the sudden surge in demand.

2   The global-warming debate has heated up since scientists discovered more evidence of the dire effects of global warming. A greater reliance on biodiesel translates into less expulsion of greenhouse gases into the atmosphere.

3   Even if there are no biodiesel distributors near you, the fuel works in any diesel engine. One small but significant step you can take is to buy a diesel car instead of a car that runs on traditional unleaded gasoline. When the "green revolution" goes into full swing, you'll be ready. In field tests, cars powered by biodiesel have been shown to perform comparably to vehicles that run on traditional fuels. Contrary to what many people believe, biodiesel is distributed all over the United States, and the number of stations where it is available is growing. There may be a biodiesel distributor coming to a town near you.

? Questions

1 What is the purpose of the list after the first paragraph?

   A. to introduce the topic of the passage

   B. to explain why biodiesel is useful

   C. to introduce the second paragraph

   D. to explain how traditional fuels work

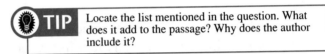

TIP Locate the list mentioned in the question. What does it add to the passage? Why does the author include it?

2 In what way is the passage intended to appeal to a wide audience?

   A. It uses technical and scientific terms.

   B. It refers to the decisions made by politicians.

   C. It tells why biodiesel is useful for everyone.

   D. It explains the upcoming "green revolution."

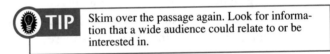

TIP Skim over the passage again. Look for information that a wide audience could relate to or be interested in.

3 If the author had included some type of graphic (e.g., a photograph, chart or map) with the passage, what type of graphic would be appropriate for the author's purpose? Explain how that type of graphic would promote or support the author's purpose. Write your answer on the lines below.

_____

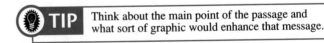

TIP Think about the main point of the passage and what sort of graphic would enhance that message.

Passage 2

Read the following passage. Then answer the questions that follow. Use the Tip below each question to help you choose the correct answer. When you finish, read the answer explanations at the end of this chapter.

Daydreams Save the Day
by Ricardo Sanchez

1   Have you ever gotten in trouble for daydreaming in class? It's not a good idea to be thinking about your new skateboard or your weekend plans when you should be learning algebra! It is rude to the instructor, and you might not learn what you need to know. However, many scientists agree that daydreaming itself is not a bad thing at all. In fact, daydreams can make your life happier and healthier in numerous ways.

2   Some psychologists (scientists who study the mind) believe that the average person daydreams for many hours each day. Critics of daydreaming say that this is a dreadful waste of time. Daydreaming usually doesn't result in any obvious progress; it is usually seen as something that keeps people from making progress. This is not really the case, however. Sometimes daydreaming can help people sort out their minds and get their ideas in order so they can think and behave more effectively. Their daydreams can make them more productive workers or students and make future progress easier.

3   There are many negative stereotypes about daydreamers, such as they are lazy and they shirk responsibilities. Although some truth may be behind the stereotypes, they definitely are not always true. Sometimes daydreams actually give people a goal to work toward. For instance, a writer might daydream about seeing his or her book in print, and that image might increase the writer's determination to keep on writing. Thus, daydreams can be a method of visualizing success in the future. Some athletes use "positive thinking" visualization while practicing. By thinking about their challenges and imagining success in the end, they tend to perform much better than athletes who have not prepared their minds.

4   A third criticism of daydreams is that too much daydreaming can make people unhappy. Of course, if a person daydreams *all day*, he or she will probably lose track of the events of real life. He or she might start to "live in the past" or in some unrealistic dream world. But for people who do a regular amount of daydreaming, the practice can make them happier. This can happen in many ways.

5   Daydreaming allows the mind to relax. Especially in stressful times, giving your mind a break is a great idea. Taking a "minivacation" by daydreaming can make a person's brain feel energized and refreshed. A brain vacation is also great for overcoming boredom. Excessive boredom can have negative effects on people and cause them to feel gloomy and tired. A little daydreaming here and there can relieve the nasty effects of boredom.

6   Many psychologists think that daydreams can also help remove fear and conflict from our lives. Like athletes who use visualizations to prepare for events, people can use daydreams to learn to deal with themselves and others. If two people are not getting along, they might be able to daydream, or visualize, ways in which they could reconcile. They might even be able to use daydreams to imagine the other's point of view and find similarities or shared interests between them. Daydreaming can help us expand our minds, and that helps us find new ways to get along with others.

7   In much the same way, people can use daydreams to ease, and even conquer, their fears. For example, if a person has a powerful fear, or phobia, of heights, he or she might imagine safely climbing higher and higher on a hill. This can prepare the person to remain calm while climbing a real hill. "Positive thinking" daydreams can strengthen a person's courage considerably. Many people have used this simple technique to conquer their phobias.

8   There are many good kinds of daydreaming that help people improve their lives. However, bad types of daydreaming exist as well. Negative daydreaming occurs most frequently in the behavior we know as "worrying." Some people get caught up in worries, and spend their days nervously picturing all sorts of frightening and embarrassing events. Worries can have a terrible effect on people's lives. Some people lie awake all night worrying, and worries and stress can weaken the body, causing people to get sick more easily.

9   One of the best ways to combat negative daydreams like worrying is to counter them with positive daydreams. Instead of worrying, people can take a more relaxed look at their problems. They can reflect on the past, imagine possibilities for the future, and then try to

decide how to handle these thoughts. By using positive daydreams and visualizations, you may well be able to overcome many kinds of negative thoughts and feelings.

10   Daydreams play an important role in our daily lives, a role that not many people stop to consider. Good daydreams can make us healthy and happy, and bad daydreams can do just the opposite. But remember—no daydreams are good daydreams in algebra class!

? Questions

4   What is the intended effect of the quotation marks placed around certain words?

   A. to show that they are often misunderstood

   B. to show that they are quoted from another source

   C. to emphasize their unimportance to the passage

   D. to indicate unusual or special terminology

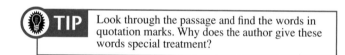

TIP Look through the passage and find the words in quotation marks. Why does the author give these words special treatment?

5   What is the purpose of the question at the beginning of the passage?

   A. to introduce the topic of daydreams

   B. to show how only students daydream

   C. to take a scientific survey of readers

   D. to ask students to be more polite

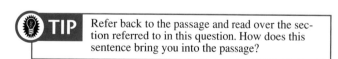

TIP Refer back to the passage and read over the section referred to in this question. How does this sentence bring you into the passage?

6   What pattern does the author use to organize the ideas in paragraphs 2 through 4?

   A. posing questions and providing answers

   B. presenting claims and arguing against them

   C. listing types of daydreams and describing them

   D. comparing and contrasting good and bad daydreams

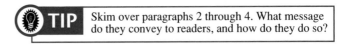 **TIP** Skim over paragraphs 2 through 4. What message do they convey to readers, and how do they do so?

7   The phrase "save the day" is a popular term that refers to someone or something rescuing others from danger or hardship. Explain why "Daydreams Save the Day" is an appropriate title for this passage. Support your explanation with three examples or details from the passage. Write your answer on the lines below.

_____

 TIP Think about the phrase "save the day" and its meaning. How does it apply to the passage you read?

Passage 3

Read the following passage. Then answer the questions that follow. Use the Tip below each question to help you choose the correct answer. When you finish, read the answer explanations at the end of this chapter.

A Rose by Any Other Name:
The Debate over the "Real" Shakespeare

1   William Shakespeare is thought to be one of the finest writers the world has even known. His sonnets, tragedies and comedies have captured the hearts and minds of readers across the globe. Although he is certainly one of literature's most beloved writers, he is also one of the most mysterious. Shakespeare both fascinates and frustrates historical scholars because very little is known about his personal life. Again and again, experts investigate the few pieces of evidence that have survived since the Elizabethan era. This probing has led many to question whether William Shakespeare wrote the plays with which he has been credited or if he even existed at all.

2   This heated debate is based on a number of inconsistencies in Shakespeare's biography. The first reason many experts question his identity is that very little historical documentation of his life exists. Even the most obscure figures in history have left some sort of paper trail investigators can follow to verify or disprove his or her existence. In Shakespeare's case, only three documents bear his signature, with various spellings of the Bard's surname, and a handful of playbills list him as an actor. No letters, journals or other type of personal correspondence support the Bard's identity as the master playwright.

3   People also list Shakespeare's background as another reason for suspicion. As the son of a community official, Shakespeare was not privy to the opportunities that existed for members of the upper class. Although little is known about his formal education, scholars of Shakespeare's work feel that the author of such plays would have needed a great knowledge of history and the ability to read both Latin and Greek. The lack of information about Shakespeare's schooling adds fuel to the debate.

4   So the question remains, if Shakespeare was not the author of some of the greatest plays ever penned, then who was? Several theories about the actual identity of the playwright exist. One of the most popular ideas is that the name William Shakespeare was a pseudonym for Edward De Vere, the seventeenth Earl of Oxford. It is thought that De Vere had to hide his true identity because many of the Shakespearean plays mock the British monarchy, with which De Vere was intimately acquainted. Opponents of this idea note that several of Shakespeare's plays were written after De Vere's death, though the dates of the plays are often disputed.

5   Other Shakespeare suspects include Sir Francis Bacon, a philosopher and lawyer, and Christopher Marlow, a famous playwright. Some claim that Mary Sidney Herbert, Countess of Pembroke, was the real author but was forced to publish under a man's name because she was a woman. Most of these people were members of the upper class or aristocracy, making them well educated and well traveled, two qualities that many feel would have been essential to the author of Shakespeare's plays.

6   However, supporters of the Bard argue that Shakespeare's social status had little to do with his abilities as a writer. They point out that many of the greatest writers in the world were self-taught and possessed raw talent rather than cultivated intellects. These supporters also look to the plays themselves to validate Shakespeare's identity. All the plays have the unique ability to transcend class and were loved by both courtiers and common people. These people believe that this supports the idea that the plays could have been written by a middle-class man.

7   Of course, until conclusive proof is discovered, the controversy over the true identity of Shakespeare will continue. Still, many people feel "the play's the thing" and that authorship has little bearing on these wonderful works.

Time Line of Shakespearean Speculation

- 1564–1616—The life of William Shakespeare

- 1728—Captain Goulding's "Essay Against Too Much Reading" suggests that Shakespeare must have had help from a trained historian to write his plays.

- 1785—James Wilmot states that the "real Shakespeare" was Sir Francis Bacon.

- 1848—American Joseph C. Hart revives the Shakespeare question and suggests Ben Jonson was the true genius.

- 1850s—Various journals print editorials and articles suggesting that different authors may have written Shakespeare's plays.

- 1890s—Literary historians suggest several other possibilities as to Shakespeare's true identity.

- 1903—Author Henry James suggests that Shakespeare was "the biggest and most successful fraud ever practiced on a patient world."

- 1900–1950—Numerous books and articles question Shakespeare's authenticity.

- Late 1900s—The Shakespeare mystery moves to television and then the Internet.

- 1987—A "Moot Court Debate" overseen by three U.S. Supreme Court justices concludes that Shakespeare probably wrote his own plays, but some arguments to the contrary are seen as very compelling.

(?) Questions

8   What pattern does the author use to organize the ideas in the passage?

   A. spatial order

   B. order of importance

   C. repetition of a key idea

   D. cause and effect

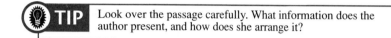

TIP   Look over the passage carefully. What information does the author present, and how does she arrange it?

9   What is the purpose of the time line at the end of the passage?

   A. to conclude the author's argument

   B. to clarify the dates given in the passage

   C. to show the development of the debate

   D. to persuade the reader to study Shakespeare

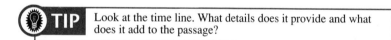

TIP   Look at the time line. What details does it provide and what does it add to the passage?

10   What is the intended effect of the list of evidence in paragraph 2?

   A. to suggest that little is known of Shakespeare

   B. to show how many people doubt Shakespeare

   C. to prove that Shakespeare was a great author

   D. to hint at Shakespeare's lasting popularity

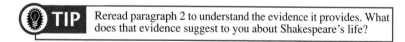

TIP   Reread paragraph 2 to understand the evidence it provides. What does that evidence suggest to you about Shakespeare's life?

11   If the author had included some type of graphic (e.g., a photograph or map) with the passage, what type of graphic would be appropriate for the author's purpose? Explain how that type of graphic would promote or support the author's purpose. Write your answer on the lines below.

TIP   Think about the passage you just read. What kind of graphic might enhance this passage?

Passage 4

Read the following passage. Then answer the questions that follow. Use the Tip below each question to help you choose the correct answer. When you finish, read the answer explanations at the end of this chapter.

MP3: Decompressed

1   Aside from the fact that MP3 players store and play music, how much do you really know about the multifarious gadgets?

What Does MP3 Stand For?

2   Though most people can explain what an MP3 file is, they usually have a difficult time with the specifics—for instance, explaining what the *M*, the *P* and the 3 represent. The MP3 format, or the technology of shrinking a music file, developed from MPEG technology, an acronym for Moving Picture Experts Group, a team of innovators who have taken on the responsibility of developing ways to store, send and view moving pictures and audio. The technology they created for sharing compressed digital video files is also called MPEG. That takes care of the *M* and *P*, but what about the 3?

3   The Moving Picture Experts Group works by creating and then enhancing digital audio and video. They group meets about three times a year to discuss their research and

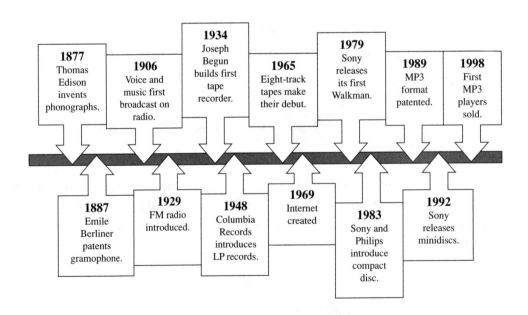

developments in the field of video compression. They first created audio layer I and audio layer II, both of which worked, except they stripped a lot of quality from music. Audio layer III allowed people to shrink music into files in which the difference in quality remains negligible.

4   So there you have it. An MP3 is really a Moving Picture Experts Group Audio Layer III file. No wonder they shortened the name.

How Much Quality Is Lost?

5   MP3 technology continues to improve, and innovators use the human ear as their inspiration. Creators of MP3 technology are masters of psychoacoustic compression, or the science of shrinking files to only include what is perceivable to the human ear.

6   The human ear can only pick up fragments of sound for two reasons. First, some tones are just imperceptible to the human ear. Second, if one instrument produces a loud sound, the human ear cannot perceive the fainter tones underlying it.

7   Scientists use a process called "perceptual noise shaping" to remove sounds from music that the human ear cannot perceive. You might notice minor differences between an analog (or traditional) recording and an MP3 file of the same song because compression removes subtleties that the human ear cannot perceive. The differences are slight when listening to MP3s on a walkman, but if you compared the playback of an MP3 file to that of an analog recording on a high-fidelity system, the difference in quality would be quite noticeable.

Just How Compressed Is an MP3?

8   Audio layer III provides a 12:1 ratio from analog to digital, which means a file is compressed to 1/12 of its original size. If you were to download one song from a CD onto your computer, it would take up about 40 million bytes (or 40 megabytes) of computer space. If you compress that music file into an MP3 file, it will only take up about 3.5 megabytes of computer space.

What's Inside My MP3 Player?

9   If you could open up your tiny music storage device, you would be amazed at everything that is going on inside! Within that slim, shiny machine are tiny parts that make music come alive. Check out this illustration of how the MPEG audio layer III coding comes out of an MP3 player as music:

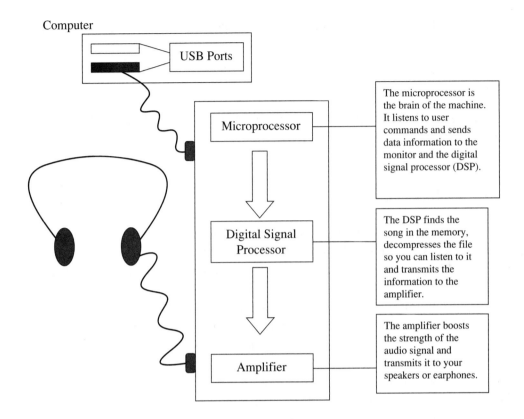

So What Should I Get?

10   There are two basic types MP3 player to choose from, each with its own advantages and disadvantages.

11   A **flash MP3 player** has no moving parts inside of it and therefore cannot store very much information (only about 200 songs). However, the flash MP3 player eliminates the problem of music skipping. These devices are very inexpensive compared with their more complex counterparts, the hard-drive MP3 players. If you want to use your device primarily for exercise, the flash MP3 player is the machine for you.

12   A **hard-drive MP3** player can have as much memory as some computers and, also like your computer, can store any type of file, not just MP3s. They also hold photos and video or text files and can be used to transport files from one computer to another. The primary benefit of a hard-drive device is the large amount of information it can store. The drawbacks are that more space means more breakable parts, a bigger price tag and a bulkier, heavier player. Finally, the music can skip if you jostle the device too much.

13   As with any purchase, you should educate yourself and then make a decision to purchase based on your personal preferences. Whichever type of player you choose, you will have a greater appreciation for the device knowing all that is going on inside!

 Questions

12 Which represents the organizational pattern of the passage?

    A. cause and effect

    B. question and answer

    C. repetition of a key idea

    D. chronological order

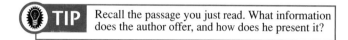

TIP | Recall the passage you just read. What information does the author offer, and how does he present it?

13 What is the purpose of the rhetorical question at the beginning of the passage?

    A. to explain how MP3 players work

    B. to test the reader's knowledge of technology

    C. to suggest that the reader learn more about MP3s

    D. to convince the reader to listen to more music

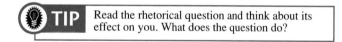

TIP | Read the rhetorical question and think about its effect on you. What does the question do?

14 In what way is the passage intended to appeal to a wide audience?

    A. It assumes everybody has an MP3 player.

    B. It shows how MP3 players can be built.

    C. It explains situations that all people experience.

    D. It gives both basic and complex information.

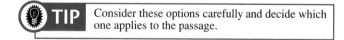

TIP | Consider these options carefully and decide which one applies to the passage.

Answers and Explanations

1   B

The first paragraph hints at many reasons why biodiesel fuel is increasingly useful to people.

2   C

To make the passage interesting and readable for all audiences, the writer tells how biodiesel may change everyone's life.

3   **Sample answer**

If the author were going to include a graphic, he or she would use a map showing the locations of biodiesel distributors in America. In the last line of the passage, the author says that a distributor might be coming to a town nearby. If the author provided a map, the reader could quickly and easily check if any nearby locations could provide this kind of fuel.

4   D

In the passage, terms like "positive thinking" and "live in the past" are put in quotations. In the context of the passage, these terms have special or unusual meanings that some readers may not be familiar with.

5   A

The author begins the passage with a question about whether the reader has ever daydreamed. This opening question introduces the topic of the passage, which is daydreaming.

6   B

In paragraphs 2 through 4, the author presents some traditional, largely negative beliefs about daydreaming and daydreamers. Then he proceeds to show why these ideas are inaccurate.

7   **Sample answer**

"Daydreams Save the Day" is an appropriate title for this selection because in the passage, the author claims that daydreams help people every day. Daydreams "save" people from boredom and keep their minds active. Daydreams also relieve conflicts and worries and help people visualize their goals.

8 D

The author uses a cause-and-effect format. First she describes Shakespeare and the lack of information about him. This lack of information is the cause of the next topic discussed in the passage: the many questions surrounding his life.

9 C

The passage talks about the Shakespeare debate, and the time line helps the text by breaking down the debate chronologically to show its development.

10 A

The author lists evidence—three signatures and a "handful" of playbills—that suggest that Shakespeare was a real person. The point of this evidence is to show that not much proof is available.

11 **Sample answer**

A series of graphics depicting the historical figures mentioned in the passage would help bring meaning to the text. For instance, a portrait of Shakespeare could be shown alongside portraits of Edward de Vere and Sir Francis Bacon. Using graphics like that would emphasize the confusion many people have about the identity of the "real" Shakespeare.

12 B

Much of this passage is organized with a series of questions (used as headings) followed by brief, informative answers to those questions.

13 C

The opening question of the passage hints that many people use MP3s but probably do not know much about their history or how they operate. With that question, the author suggests that the reader read on to find this knowledge.

14 D

This passage appeals to many kinds of readers because it gives basic information (e.g., what an MP3 player is, what MP3 files are) and then works up to more advanced information.

Section 2
Writing

Chapter 8

Writing an Essay

Benchmarks

Writing Applications

C. Produce letters (e.g., business letters, letters to the editor, job applications) that follow the conventional style appropriate to the text, include appropriate details and exclude extraneous details and inconsistencies.

E. Write a persuasive piece that states a clear position, includes relevant information and offers compelling evidence in the form of facts and details.

Grade Level Indicators

3. Write business letters, letters to the editor and job applications that do the following:

   a. Address audience needs, stated purpose and context in a clear and efficient manner

   b. Follow the conventional style appropriate to the text, using proper technical terms

   c. Include appropriate facts and details

   d. Exclude extraneous details and inconsistencies

   e. Provide a sense of closure to the writing

4. Write informational essays or reports, including research, that do the following:

   a. Pose relevant and tightly drawn questions that engage the reader

   b. Provide a clear and accurate perspective on the subject

   c. Create an organizing structure appropriate to the purpose, audience and context

   d. Support the main ideas with facts, details, examples and explanations from sources

   e. Document sources and include bibliographies

5. Write persuasive compositions that do the following:

   a. Support arguments with detailed evidence

   b. Exclude irrelevant information

   c. Cite sources of information

Writing Conventions

A. Use correct spelling conventions.

B. Use correct punctuation and capitalization.

C. Demonstrate understanding of the grammatical conventions of the English language.

Grade Level Indicators

1. Use correct spelling conventions.

2. Use correct capitalization and punctuation.

3. Use clauses (e.g., main, subordinate) and phrases (e.g., gerund, infinitive, participial).

4. Use parallel structure to present items in a series and items juxtaposed for emphasis.

5. Use proper placement of modifiers.

Introduction

Section 2 of this book helps you prepare for the OGT in writing. The test includes two writing prompts, ten multiple-choice questions and one short-response question. In this chapter, you will learn how to write an essay in response to a writing prompt. Writing prompts on the OGT might be expository, meaning they may ask you to describe or explain something, or they might be persuasive. In a persuasive essay, you will need to convince the reader to believe as you believe.

For the second part of the OGT in writing, covered in Chapter 9, you will answer multiple-choice and short-response questions associated with brief paragraphs or sentences. Some of the questions are clustered together, while others stand alone. Many of the questions will ask you to choose the best way to edit errors or organize information based on the given paragraphs or sentences. Each multiple-choice question will have four answer options. For short-response questions, you will have to write your answer on the lines provided in the answer booklet.

OGT Writing Prompts

The OGT will ask you to write two essays in response to writing prompts: one at the beginning of the test and one at the end of the test. The writing prompts you respond to will be expository or persuasive. To complete these essays, you will do some prewriting, drafting and revising. You will have a maximum of 150 minutes (2½ hours) to complete the entire writing test, including both writing prompts and the multiple-choice and short-response questions.

Expository Prompt

An expository prompt asks you to define, explain or tell how to do something. The following is an example of an expository writing prompt:

> **Most people have a favorite season or time of year. Write an essay describing your favorite season. Discuss what makes that season special to you.**

Persuasive Prompt

A persuasive prompt asks you to convince the reader to accept your opinion or to take a specific action. The following is an example of a persuasive writing prompt:

> **To cut back on expenses, your principal has asked the school board for permission to cancel all field trips for the remainder of the year. Some people think this is a good idea because they consider a field trip a "vacation" from learning and therefore an unnecessary expense. Write to the school board explaining your position on the issue. Use facts and examples to develop your argument.**

For each of the two writing prompts on the OGT, you will be given a blank page on which to plan your answer. Your response on this planning sheet will not be graded. Once you have planned your essay, you will have four pages on which to write the final version. The final version of your essay will be graded.

Hints for Taking the OGT in Writing

- Read the prompt carefully.
- Plan your writing by organizing your ideas.
- Support your ideas by providing details about each event, reason or argument.
- Use various sentence structures.
- Choose words that help others understand what you mean.
- Review and edit your writing.

Developing Your Essay

As you begin to develop each essay, remember the three stages of writing: prewriting, drafting and revising. Whether you are responding to an expository prompt or a persuasive prompt, you should always begin by prewriting. Think about the audience you will be writing for and the purpose of your writing. Are you being asked to explain something to readers or convince them of something? Once you have determined your central idea, purpose and audience, jot down some supporting details and organize or outline your ideas into a logical sequence. Then begin the drafting stage.

In the drafting stage, you will write a rough version of your work. The most important thing to remember when writing your draft is simply to get all your ideas down on paper. This stage of your writing does not have to be perfect. It is acceptable for the rough draft to have mistakes. You can fix your mistakes and make any necessary changes in the final stage of writing: revising.

When your rough draft is finished, begin revising and editing your work. Read your rough draft carefully. Look for mistakes in grammar, spelling, punctuation and capitalization. Look for sentence fragments. Make sure that you have stated your main idea or that you have provided enough supporting details for readers to determine the central theme. Reword sentences or move entire paragraphs to make your writing flow in a clear, logical order. Add more details to make your writing vibrant and exciting. When you are happy with your revised draft, write the final copy of your work on the Answer Sheet.

Content and Organization

Your composition should be framed by strong opening and closing ideas. Make sure that you have addressed the reasons your topic is important and have presented a conclusion stating why you feel as you do about your topic.

Between the opening and closing of your composition are your main ideas and supporting details. Make sure that your ideas are clear and that you have included several supporting details rather than simply stressing the same point multiple times. Your ideas should follow a logical progression; that is, your transitions from one main idea to another should be smooth, not choppy, flowing easily from one idea to the next. Your ideas should also be supported by details, or reasons why you believe your ideas to be true. In addition, be sure that you make smooth transitions from the opening of your essay to the main ideas to the closing.

Sentence Construction

Make sure that you follow traditional grammar rules when composing sentences. Check to ensure that you have placed periods and commas in logical places. Also make sure that all your sentences are not structured the same way. Variety will make your composition more interesting and more effective.

Usage

When you revise and edit, be sure to check that you have used correct verb tenses and agreements. For example, if you are writing about something that happened in the past, make certain that all the verbs you use to describe the past event are set in the past tense. Also, look at your pronouns (*I, you, he, she, it, we, they*) to make sure you have used them correctly. Examine your composition to verify that you have used words that will engage your audience. If you do not like the look or sound of a certain word in your composition, try to replace it with a better one.

Mechanics

Mechanics are the spelling, capitalization and punctuation in your composition. You are not permitted to use reference materials such as dictionaries and style manuals during the OGT, so you will need to draw on your own knowledge to use correct mechanics.

How Essays Are Graded

The OGT in writing is worth a total of 48 points. The multiple-choice and short-response section of the test is worth 12 points. You earn the remaining 36 points through your responses to the writing prompts. It is important that you give yourself enough time to respond to both writing prompts as completely and correctly as possible. They are worth 75 percent of your total score on the writing portion of the OGT.

The essays you write for the OGT are scored independently by two readers using two scoring rubrics. Each reader uses the writing applications rubric to evaluate your essay for its overall quality and then assigns it a score from 0 to 6 based on the specific scoring guidelines. Each reader also uses the writing conventions rubric to evaluate spelling, capitalization, punctuation and grammar in your essay and then assigns it a score of 0 to 3. The final score is the sum of both sets of scores from both readers. Therefore, a perfect essay would receive a score of 18 points: 6 points from each reader for writing applications and 3 points from each reader for writing conventions. The following scoring rubrics outline how your essays will be scored.

Writing Applications Rubric

Score	Description
6	This is a superior piece of writing. The prompt is directly addressed, and the response is adapted effectively to audience and purpose. It is exceptionally developed, containing compelling ideas, examples and details. The response, using a clearly evident organizational plan, actively engages the reader with a unified and coherent sequence and structure of ideas. The response consistently uses a variety of sentence structures, effective word choices and an engaging style.
5	This is an excellent piece of writing. The prompt is directly addressed and the response is clearly adapted to audience and purpose. It is very well developed, containing compelling ideas, examples and details. The response, using a clearly evident organizational plan, engages the reader with a unified and coherent sequence and structure of ideas. The response typically uses a variety of sentence structures, effective word choices and an engaging style.
4	This is an effective piece of writing. While the prompt is addressed and the response adapts to audience and purpose, there are occasional inconsistencies in the response's overall plan. The response is well developed, containing effective ideas, examples and details. The response, using a good organizational plan, presents the reader with a generally unified and coherent sequence and structure of ideas. The response often uses a variety of sentence structures, appropriate word choices and an effective style.
3	This is an adequate piece of writing. While the prompt is generally addressed and the response shows an awareness of audience and purpose, there are inconsistencies in the response's overall plan. Although the response contains ideas, examples and details, they are repetitive, unevenly developed and occasionally inappropriate. The response, using an acceptable organizational plan, presents the reader with a generally unified and coherent sequence and structure of ideas. The response occasionally uses a variety of sentence structures, appropriate word choices and an effective style.
2	This is a marginal piece of writing. While an attempt is made to address the prompt, the response shows at best an inconsistent awareness of audience and purpose. When ideas, examples and details are present, they are frequently repetitive, unevenly developed and occasionally inappropriate. The response, using a limited organizational plan, does not present the reader with a generally unified and coherent sequence and structure of ideas. The response is exemplified by noticeable lapses in sentence structure, use of appropriate word choices and a clear, readable style.

1	This is an inadequate piece of writing. There is a weak attempt made to address the prompt. The response shows little or no awareness of audience and purpose. There is little or no development of ideas or the response is limited to paraphrasing the prompt. There is little or no evidence of organizational structure. The response is exemplified by severe lapses in sentence structure, use of appropriate word choices and a clear, readable style.
0	The following are categories of papers that cannot be scored: off task (complete disregard for the writing task identified by the prompt), completely illegible, in a language other than English, or no response.

Writing Conventions Rubric

Score	Description
3	The written response is free from errors that impair a reader's understanding and comprehension. Few errors, if any, are present in capitalization, punctuation and spelling. The writing displays a consistent understanding of grammatical conventions.
2	Occasional errors may impair a reader's understanding of the written response. Some capitalization, punctuation and spelling errors are present. The writing displays some understanding of grammatical conventions.
1	Errors are frequent and impair a reader's understanding of the written response. Numerous errors in capitalization, punctuation and spelling are present. The writing displays a minimal understanding of grammatical conventions.
0	The following are categories of papers that cannot be scored: completely illegible, in a language other than English, or no response; OR the length and complexity of the response is insufficient to demonstrate the writer has control over standard English conventions.

Sample Essays

Remember the writing prompts you read in the beginning of this chapter? The following are sample 6-point responses to those prompts. Notice that the samples clearly respond to the prompt. They contain good opening and closing statements and progress logically from beginning to end. The essays are well developed and stay focused on the topic throughout. They contain few, if any, errors in usage, sentence construction and mechanics.

Expository Prompt

Most people have a favorite season or time of year. Write an essay describing your favorite season. Discuss what makes this season special to you.

Sample Answer

My favorite season of the year is autumn. In autumn, the hot, humid summer air turns cool and crisp. The forest behind my house begins to change color. The lush greens of summer become an array of warm autumn hues like red, orange, brown and gold. When the sun shines through the trees, it looks like the forest is a great fire trying to warm the gray sky. As I ride my bike through the countryside, fields are dotted with bright orange pumpkins, and bright red apples hang from trees, ready for picking. At night, the temperature drops dramatically and I can see my breath in the air. The smell of wood smoke from the chimneys of neighboring houses fills the air. On my porch, I listen to the sounds of the woods—twigs cracking in the dark blanket of the night forest and a light breeze scraping fallen leaves across the paved driveway. I snuggle deeper into a wool blanket to keep off the chill of a potential frost, and I sip warm apple cider with my family.

These tastes, sounds, smells and sights of fall are special to me because I know that winter is on its way. I know that soon my family will be curled up on cozy couches next to a blazing fire. My house will take on new warmth; not the hot, sticky air of summer but the warmth you feel when you come in from the cold.

Persuasive Prompt

To cut back on expenses, your principal has asked the school board for permission to cancel all field trips for the remainder of the year. Some people think this is a good idea because they consider a field trip a "vacation" from learning and therefore an unnecessary expense. Write to the school board explaining your position on the issue. Use facts and examples to develop your argument.

Sample Answer

Dear School Board:

I am aware that you were recently contacted by Mr. Henry, principal of Westmore High School, regarding permission to cancel the school's field trips for the rest of the year. Although I understand the need to conserve school money to stay within the fixed budget, I am convinced that we can find alternative sources of funding without having to cancel our field trips.

Some people, such as Mr. Henry, think that field trips are vacations from learning. I understand how some people might make this mistake. Students get to take a break from the monotony of a school day, get on a bus and travel to a theater, an art museum, a science center or a historical site. They get to watch plays, see magnificent works of art, try new inventions or experience life as it was in the past. These are all fun activities that some might view as purely recreational.

What people seem to forget, however, is that these field trips do not allow us to take a vacation from our education. Rather, field trips enhance what we have learned in the classroom. Although books, chalkboards and lectures are important, hands-on learning gives students the opportunity to take what they have learned and see how it is applied in real life. Why silently read a play when you can see it performed live? Why study paintings in a book when you can look at them in person? Why study pictures of the parts of a flower when you can visit a greenhouse and study the real thing? Field trips provide us with not only a break from the monotony of a regular school day but also a chance to supplement what we learn in the classroom with hands-on experiences.

For these reasons, it is my belief that funding for field trips should not be cut. Instead, maybe we could augment our budget in other ways, such as bake sales or parental donations. If we in this educational community put our heads together, I am sure we can come up with a better solution for our students. Thank you for taking the time to consider my thoughts on this issue.

Sincerely,

Patrick Grier

Chapter 9

Revising and Editing

Benchmarks

Writing Processes

A. Formulate writing ideas and identify a topic appropriate to the purpose and audience.

B. Determine the usefulness of organizers and apply appropriate prewriting tasks.

C. Use revision strategies to improve the style, variety of sentence structure, clarity of the controlling idea, logic, effectiveness of word choice and transitions between paragraphs, passages or ideas.

D. Edit to improve sentence fluency, grammar and usage.

E. Apply tools to judge the quality of writing.

Grade Level Indicators

2. Determine the usefulness of and apply appropriate prewriting tasks (e.g., background reading, interviews or surveys).

3. Establish and develop a clear thesis statement for informational writing or a clear plan or outline for narrative writing.

4. Determine a purpose and audience and plan strategies (e.g., adapting focus, content structure and point of view) to address purpose and audience.

5. Use organizational strategies (e.g., notes, outlines) to plan writing.

6. Organize writing to create a coherent whole with an effective and engaging introduction, body and conclusion, and a closing sentence that summarizes, extends or elaborates on points or ideas in the writing.

7. Use a variety of sentence structures and lengths (e.g., simple, compound and complex sentences; parallel or repetitive sentence structure).

8. Use paragraph form in writing, including topic sentences that arrange paragraphs in a logical sequence, using effective transitions and closing sentences and maintaining coherence across the whole through the use of parallel structures.

9. Use language, including precise nouns, action verbs, sensory details and colorful modifiers, and style that are appropriate to audience and purpose, and use techniques to convey a personal style and voice.

11. Reread and analyze clarity of writing, consistency of point of view and effectiveness of organizational structure.

12. Add and delete information and details to better elaborate on stated central idea and more effectively accomplish purpose.

13. Rearrange words, sentences and paragraphs, and add transitional words and phrases to clarify meaning and maintain consistent style, tone and voice.

15. Proofread writing, edit to improve conventions (e.g., grammar, spelling, punctuation and capitalization), identify and correct fragments and run-ons, and eliminate inappropriate slang or informal language.

Introduction

In addition to writing essays in response to expository or persuasive writing prompts, you will be asked several multiple-choice questions and one short-response question on the OGT in writing. A few of these questions will be about outlines and excerpts from handbooks. Other questions will be based on paragraphs or sentences that require edits and revisions. Some of these questions will ask you to choose a sentence that should be inserted into an essay or to choose the best transition between sentences in an essay. Others will ask you to choose the best topic sentence for a paragraph. You will also be asked a few questions about punctuation and capitalization. The short-response question may ask you to write a paragraph based on some notes about a specific topic.

Hints for Taking the Multiple-Choice and Short-Response Portions of the OGT in Writing

- Think positively. Some questions may seem hard, but others will be easy.

- Relax and do your best.

- Learn how to answer each kind of question. Some questions on the OGT in writing have four answer choices from which to choose, and others require you to provide a short response.

- Read the directions carefully. Ask your teacher to explain any directions you do not understand.

- Read the questions very carefully.

- First answer the questions you are sure about. If a question seems too difficult, skip it and go back to it later.

- Be sure to fill in each answer circle completely. Do not make any stray marks on the answer sheet.

- Check each answer to make sure it is the best answer for the question.

Revision Practice for the OGT in Writing

The following are examples of revision questions that will be asked on the OGT in writing. Read each question, and then use the Tip below each question to help you choose the correct answer. When you finish, read the answer explanations at the end of this chapter.

 **Questions**

Read the following outline and answer question 1.

Outline for Booklet on Using a Digital Camera

   I. Introduction

      A. Table of Contents

      B. Getting to Know the Camera (Diagram 1)

      C. Installing Camera Memory Card (Diagram 2)

  II. Basic Camera Operation

      A. Charging the Camera's Batteries

      B. Choosing the Right Mode

      C. Taking a Picture

      D. Saving a Picture

 III. Transferring Pictures to a Computer

 IV. Using Computer Software to Enhance Pictures

1   In which section of the outline would you find the following sentence?

By selecting the Sport setting, you guarantee that even fast-moving subjects will remain in focus while you snap the picture.

  A. Section IA

  B. Section IB

  C. Section IIB

  D. Section III

 Look at each section of the outline listed in the answer choices. Where would you most likely find information about choosing the right setting to take a picture?

Use the following information from a handbook on language to answer question 2.

- Capitalize races, nationalities, languages, and religions: We ordered Chinese food.

- Capitalize words that indicate particular sections of the country: During the Civil War, the *North* fought against the *South*.

- Capitalize the names of specific bodies of water: The airplane flew over the *Pacific Ocean*.

2   Which is the correct way to edit the sentence below?

While vacationing in the southeast, we visited a town settled by Spanish explorers in 1565 and went to a beach on the Atlantic Ocean.

A. While vacationing in the Southeast, we visited a town settled by spanish explorers in 1565 and went to a beach on the Atlantic Ocean.

B. While vacationing in the Southeast, we visited a town settled by Spanish explorers in 1565 and went to a beach on the Atlantic ocean.

C. While vacationing in the Southeast, we visited a town settled by Spanish explorers in 1565 and went to a beach on the Atlantic Ocean.

D. While vacationing in the southeast, we visited a town settled by Spanish explorers in 1565 and went to a beach on the Atlantic ocean.

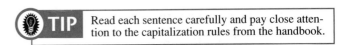 Read each sentence carefully and pay close attention to the capitalization rules from the handbook.

3   Select the correct way to edit the sentence.

Next Saturday we will wash the car, attending a birthday party and go to the movies.

A. Next Saturday, we will wash the car, attending a birthday party and go to the movies.

B. Next Saturday, we will wash the car, attend a birthday party and go to the movies.

C. Next Saturday we washing the car, attending a birthday party and going to the movies.

D. Next Saturday we will wash the car, will attend a birthday party and going to the movies.

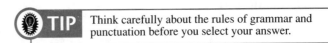 Think carefully about the rules of grammar and punctuation before you select your answer.

4   You have been given the assignment to speak about Neil Armstrong at an assembly in your high school. Use the information below to organize and write the introduction. Your introduction should be in paragraph form.

Neil Armstrong

- Was born in Wapakoneta, Ohio, in 1930
- Attended Purdue University and the University of Southern California
- Flew as an aviator in the Navy before becoming an astronaut
- Served as commander of the *Apollo 11* mission to the moon in 1969
- Was the first person to set foot on the moon
- Said of the moon landing, "That's one small step for [a] man, one giant leap for mankind"
- Went on to become a professor

 TIP As you write your answer, be sure to include all the bulleted points listed. On the OGT in writing, you will not have to keep the information in the same order, but you will have to mention each point to receive full credit for your answer.

Read the draft paragraph and then answer question 5.

¹ I was in fifth grade when my cousin Sara moved away. ² We had been not only cousins but also best friends and next-door neighbors. ³ It was hard not having Sara around. ⁴ I soon learned that we could still remain close by calling and writing to each other.

5   In the context of the paragraph, which transition would be appropriate to use at the beginning of sentence 4?

A. Meanwhile, I soon learned that we could still remain close by calling and writing to each other.

B. Therefore, I soon learned that we could still remain close by calling and writing to each other.

C. Unfortunately, I soon learned that we could still remain close by calling and writing to each other.

D. However, I soon learned that we could still remain close by calling and writing to each other.

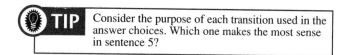 **TIP** Consider the purpose of each transition used in the answer choices. Which one makes the most sense in sentence 5?

Answers and Explanations

1 B

Descriptions of different settings on the camera would most likely be found in the section of the booklet called "Choosing the Right Mode." You can tell from the title that the section explains the best time to use each setting.

2 C

This is the only sentence that demonstrates correct capitalization of a region in the country, a nationality and a body of water.

3 B

Answer choice B is the only sentence that is grammatically correct. There should be a comma after the introductory phrase "Next Saturday," and each part of the compound predicate should agree with the subject.

4 **Sample answer**

I would like to welcome everyone to today's special assembly, where we will share stories about our personal heroes. I will start things off by telling you about my personal hero, Neil Armstrong.

Perhaps best known as the first person to set foot on the moon, Armstrong was born in Wapakoneta, Ohio, in 1930. He attended Purdue University and the University of Southern California. He also served as an aviator in the Navy. Later, he became an astronaut and, in 1969, commanded the *Apollo 11* mission to the moon. On taking his first steps on the moon, Armstrong commented, "That's one small step for [a] man, one giant leap for mankind." After his successful Apollo mission, Armstrong went on to become a professor. However, his accomplishments as an astronaut will never be forgotten.

5 D

In this case, the writer is making a contrast. Sara's moving away was difficult for the writer, but it was made easier by their calls and letters. The transition word *however* is often used to indicate that a contrast is being made. Answer choice D is correct.

OHIO GRADUATION TESTS

Reading

Practice Test 1

PRACTICE TEST 1: READING

Each passage in this test is followed by several questions. After reading the passage, choose the correct answer for each multiple-choice question, and then mark the corresponding circle on the Answer Sheet. If you change an answer, be sure to erase the first mark completely.

For each written-response question, answer completely in the space provided. You may not need to use the entire space.

You may refer to the passages as often as necessary. Make sure the number of the question in this book corresponds to the number on the Answer Sheet. Be sure all your answers are complete.

The Yellowed Pages of a Newspaper

1   Have you ever stood in line at the grocery store and rifled through the periodicals near the cash register? You might see some ordinary newspapers and maybe a few glossy fashion or home-decorating magazines. The headlines most likely to grab your attention, however, belong to the tabloids. These publications, which often contain stories about unidentified flying objects, alien babies or celebrities who have returned from the dead, all have one thing in common: sensationalism. Tabloids tend to focus on stories of the bizarre, the unexplainable or the extraordinary. While these stories may be intriguing and suspenseful, they are usually quickly dismissed by readers and are certainly not considered good, concrete journalism. The sensationalistic—and sometimes even <u>fabricated</u>—stories in these types of publications are often referred to as "yellow journalism." Believe it or not, yellow journalism actually began in the late nineteenth century with a competition between two of the leading daily newspapers in New York.

2   Though today his name is associated with the most prestigious award in American journalism, the Pulitzer Prize, Joseph Pulitzer was one of the men responsible for the creation of yellow journalism. Pulitzer was the owner of one of New York's most successful dailies, the *New York World*. The paper's bold headlines and flamboyant approach to the news appealed

Go to next page

to many readers, including women, immigrants and the poor. The ideas and opinions of these groups were often overshadowed in the other, more conservative newspapers. The Sunday edition of the *New York World* even included a colorful comic strip called "Hogan's Alley," which featured a popular character whose bright yellow clothing earned him the name the Yellow Kid.

3   The success of the *New York World* led other newspaper owners to imitate Pulitzer's daring new format. Among them was the owner of the *San Francisco Examiner*, William Randolph Hearst. As a student at Harvard, Hearst had worked on the university's newspaper. Upon leaving school, Hearst decided to make journalism his life's work. To prepare for his chosen career, he served as an apprentice to Pulitzer at the *World*. Within a year, he had acquired his own newspaper, the struggling *San Francisco Examiner*, from his father. However, using Pulitzer's format, Hearst managed to transform the troubled paper into the best-selling newspaper in San Francisco.

4   After achieving success in California, Hearst set his sights on a new challenge: owning the top daily newspaper in New York. In 1895, he purchased the *New York Journal*, another small publication fighting to survive in the competitive New York market. Under Hearst's leadership, the *Journal* quickly became the *New York World*'s biggest competition. In an effort to boost circulation, Hearst once again applied the bold approach to the news he had learned from Pulitzer. The headlines grew bigger and bolder, and the stories became more sensational and suspenseful. Hearst lowered the price of the paper to just one penny, which even the poorest citizens of New York City could afford. In an even bolder move, Hearst enticed most of the staff of Pulitzer's *World*, including the creator of the "Hogan's Alley" comic strip, Richard Outcault, to leave their positions and work for the *Journal*.

5   Not to be outdone, Pulitzer replaced Outcault with a new artist to continue the "Hogan's Alley" comic strip. Conservative daily newspapers in New York witnessed the battle of the Yellow Kids and <u>dubbed</u> Hearst and Pulitzer's brand of reporting "yellow journalism." The term remains in use today to describe journalism that relies on glaring headlines and sensationalistic stories to sell subscriptions.

Go to next page

6 Perhaps the height of yellow journalism occurred during the Cuban Revolution, which eventually led to the Spanish-American War. Most newspapers try to approach the news objectively. They provide both sides of the story and let readers decide for themselves which side is right. However, Hearst's *Journal* clearly stated its support for the Cuban revolutionaries fighting for their freedom from Spain. The *Journal's* stories about the injustices committed against Cuban citizens by the Spanish government supplied American readers with the scandalous material they had come to crave.

7 At the same time, the competition between Hearst and Pulitzer was growing fiercer, and neither man was willing to lose. In efforts to outdo each other, Hearst and Pulitzer did whatever they could to sell the most newspapers. They often lifted news right from the pages of their competitors. This practice would eventually contribute to the demise of Pulitzer's *New York World*. In 1898, Hearst caught Pulitzer in the act of stealing news from his newspaper. Hearst placed a fabricated story in the *Journal* about the death of Colonel Reflipe W. Thenuz, which was a crafty juggling of the phrase, "We pilfer the news." The next day, the details of Thenuz's death were recounted in the pages of Pulitzer's *New York World*. This gave Hearst the ammunition he needed to sink the *World's* reputation.

8 Of course, Pulitzer wasn't the only yellow journalist guilty of questionable practices. According to legend, Hearst sent an illustrator to Cuba to capture the struggles of the Cuban citizens as they fought against Spanish control. Upon arriving, the illustrator sent a cable to Hearst explaining that there was no war to cover. Supposedly, Hearst responded with his own cable: "You furnish the pictures. I'll furnish the war." Hearst denied that this transmission ever took place, but it has long been included in discussions of yellow journalism.

9 As the problems in Cuba escalated, the *New York Journal* and the *New York World* continued their sensationalistic coverage, the height of which came when the American ship *Maine* blew up in a Cuban harbor. The military cautioned against jumping to conclusions, but both the *Journal* and the *World* placed the blame for the explosion on Spain. They called for President William McKinley to declare war. The military eventually determined that the *Maine's* explosion was in fact caused by outside forces, and the United States declared war on Spain on April 25, 1898.

Go to next page

10   Many people feel that without the pressure of the yellow press, the United States would not have entered into the war with Spain. Some have gone so far as to call it the "Newspapers' War." While newspapers may have fueled public opinion of the war, they certainly were not solely responsible for the United States government's decision to declare war on Spain. Nonetheless, the Cuban Revolution, the Spanish-American War and yellow journalism will forever share a historical link, as will Hearst and Pulitzer.

1   Give three examples of how William Randolph Hearst made the *Journal* as popular as the *World*, and explain how each example was different from the practices of most newspapers of the day. Write your answer in the space provided. (4 points)

2   "The sensationalistic—and sometimes even <u>fabricated</u>—stories in these types of publications are often referred to as 'yellow journalism.'"

In this excerpt from the passage, the word <u>fabricated</u> means

A.   written.

B.   exciting.

C.   fictional.

D.   colorful.

3   "Conservative daily newspapers in New York witnessed the battle of the Yellow Kids and <u>dubbed</u> Hearst and Pulitzer's brand of reporting 'yellow journalism.'"

In this excerpt from the passage, the word <u>dubbed</u> means

A.   changed.

B.   termed.

C.   adapted.

D.   expanded.

Go to next page

4 Which sentence summarizes the purpose of paragraphs 3 and 4 in the passage?

    A. They explain how Hearst made two struggling papers successful.

    B. They show how one newspaper stole headlines from another.

    C. They tell how Hearst worked at his college newspaper.

    D. They reveal how Hearst acquired a newspaper from his father.

5 Which idea from the passage is an example of irony?

    A. Hearst caught Joseph Pulitzer stealing headlines from his newspaper.

    B. A prestigious prize is named for someone who helped start yellow journalism.

    C. Hearst worked at a university newspaper and then acquired his own newspaper.

    D. The artist of "Hogan's Alley" worked for both Pulitzer and Hearst.

6 What is the main purpose of this passage?

    A. to entertain readers with a story about successful newspaper owners

    B. to persuade readers to read newspapers on a regular basis

    C. to convince readers that journalists were responsible for starting a war

    D. to inform readers about a form of journalism that relied on sensationalism

7 According to the article, what was the main reason people enjoyed reading Hearst's and Pulitzer's newspapers?

    A. They were eloquent.

    B. They were inexpensive.

    C. They were thrilling.

    D. They were colorful.

Go to next page

8   Which quote illustrates compare-and-contrast organization?

   A.   "Perhaps the height of yellow journalism occurred during the Cuban Revolution, which eventually led to the Spanish-American War."

   B.   "The ideas and opinions of these groups were often overshadowed by other, more conservative newspapers."

   C.   "As a student at Harvard, Hearst had worked on the university's newspaper."

   D.   "Upon arriving, the illustrator sent a cable to Hearst explaining that there was no war to cover."

9   What is the intended effect of the quote in paragraph 8, when Hearst tells his illustrator, "You furnish the pictures. I'll furnish the war"?

   A.   Hearst wanted to fight in a war and have his illustrator write about it.

   B.   Hearst wanted to start a war so he would be able to report on it.

   C.   Hearst needed to get his illustrator away from the war and out of danger.

   D.   Hearst intended to fabricate a war so that he would have a story.

10 Summarize paragraph 3. Write your answer in the space provided. (2 points)

Excerpt from *Narrative of the Life of Frederick Douglass*

by Frederick Douglass

1   I was born in Tuckahoe, near Hillsborough, and about twelve miles from Easton, in Talbot County, Maryland. I have no accurate knowledge of my age, never having seen any authentic record containing it. By far the larger part of the slaves know as little of their ages as horses know of theirs, and it is the wish of most masters within my knowledge to keep their slaves thus ignorant. I do not remember to have ever met a slave who could tell of his birthday. They seldom come nearer to it than planting-time, harvest-time, cherry-time, spring-time, or fall-time. A want of information concerning my own was a source of unhappiness to me even during childhood. The white children could tell their ages. I could not tell why I ought to be <u>deprived</u> of the same privilege. I was not allowed to make any inquiries of my master concerning it. He deemed all such inquiries on the part of a slave improper and <u>impertinent</u>, and evidence of a restless spirit. The nearest estimate I can give makes me now between twenty-seven and twenty-eight years of age. I come to this, from hearing my master say, some time during 1835, I was about seventeen years old. . . .

2   My mother and I were separated when I was but an infant—before I knew her as my mother. It is a common custom, in the part of Maryland from which I ran away, to part children from their mothers at a very early age. Frequently, before the child has reached its twelfth month, its mother is taken from it, and hired out on some farm a considerable distance off, and the child is placed under the care of an old woman, too old for field labor. For what this separation is done, I do not know, unless it be to hinder the development of the child's affection toward its mother, and to blunt and destroy the natural affection of the mother for the child. This is the inevitable result.

Go to next page

3   I never saw my mother, to know her as such, more than four or five times in my life; and each of these times was very short in duration, and at night. She was hired by a Mr. Stewart, who lived about twelve miles from my home. She made her journeys to see me in the night, travelling the whole distance on foot, after the performance of her day's work. She was a field hand, and a whipping is the penalty of not being in the field at sunrise, unless a slave has special permission from his or her master to the contrary—a permission which they seldom get, and one that gives to him that gives it the proud name of being a kind master. I do not recollect of ever seeing my mother by the light of day. She was with me in the night. She would lie down with me, and get me to sleep, but long before I waked she was gone. Very little communication ever took place between us. Death soon ended what little we could have while she lived, and with it her hardships and suffering. She died when I was about seven years old, on one of my master's farms, near Lee's Mill. I was not allowed to be present during her illness, at her death, or burial. She was gone long before I knew anything about it. Never having enjoyed, to any considerable extent, her soothing presence, her tender and watchful care, I received the tidings of her death with much the same emotions I should have probably felt at the death of a stranger. . . .

4   I have had two masters. My first master's name was Anthony. I do not remember his first name. He was generally called Captain Anthony—a title which, I presume, he acquired by sailing a craft on the Chesapeake Bay. He was not considered a rich slaveholder. He owned two or three farms, and about thirty slaves. His farms and slaves were under the care of an overseer. The overseer's name was Plummer. Mr. Plummer was a miserable drunkard, a profane swearer, and a savage monster. He always went armed with a cowskin and a heavy cudgel. I have known him to cut and slash the women's heads so horribly, that even master would be enraged at his cruelty, and would threaten to whip him if he did not mind himself. Master, however, was not a humane slaveholder. It required extraordinary barbarity on the part of an overseer to affect him. He was a cruel man, hardened by a long life of slaveholding. He would at times seem to take great pleasure in whipping a slave. . . . No words, no tears, no prayers, from his gory victim, seemed to move his iron heart from its bloody purpose. . . . It was a most terrible spectacle. I wish I could commit to paper the feelings with which I beheld it.

Go to next page

11 The main conflict in this story is between

     A.   the narrator and his mother.

     B.   the master and the overseer.

     C.   the narrator and his memories.

     D.   the overseer and the slaves.

12 How does the narrator feel about his childhood?

     A.   He is frustrated that he does not know his age and barely remembers his mother.

     B.   He is proud that he left the bonds of slavery to become an educated young man.

     C.   He is ashamed that he was raised as a slave and does not want anyone to know.

     D.   He is angry that his master would not let him be with his mother when she got sick.

13 Which might be an appropriate subtitle for the story?

     A.   A Splendid Birth

     B.   Cruelty Amidst Cotton Crops

     C.   Misty Memories of Mother

     D.   An Emotionless Era

14 "He deemed all such inquiries on the part of a slave improper and <u>impertinent</u>." (paragraph 1)

Which word represents the meaning of <u>impertinent</u>?

     A.   unnecessary

     B.   disrespectful

     C.   conscientious

     D.   inconvenient

15 Using four references from the passage, describe aspects of the narrator's past life as a slave that are disturbing to him. Write your answer in the space provided. (4 points)

16 The mother's nighttime visits with the narrator can be viewed as a metaphor for

A. the narrator's lack of knowledge about his roots.

B. the mother's reluctance to see her son.

C. the narrator's inquiries about the year of his birth.

D. the mother's status as a suffering field hand.

17 Why does the mother walk twelve miles to visit the narrator?

A. to tell him stories about his childhood

B. to make sure that he is being treated properly

C. to provide him with what affection she can

D. to let him know that she is getting sick

18 Explain the importance of conflict to the development of the story. Give two examples or pieces of information from the story to support your explanation. Write your answer in the space provided. (2 points)

19 As used in paragraph 1, a person who has been <u>deprived</u> of something is

A. destitute.

B. disadvantaged.

C. underdeveloped.

D. unhappy.

Go to next page

All About the Music

1   While they waited impatiently to go on stage, Shaz and Zoë rehearsed their tra-la-las in the hallway, preparing their voices for the concert. As usual, Sela was panicking: pacing, sweating, sucking on mentholated cough drops to soothe her throat and reciting the lyrics repeatedly.

2   Lost in anxiety, Sela bumped into Jorge, and despite her oblivious stare, Jorge asked if she was excited for the band's performance. His dad worked at the Roxy Club and had arranged for Sela's band to play that night. Sela had pleaded with him for the opportunity, but now that it was happening, she was beyond petrified.

3   When Jorge asked Sela what was bothering her, Sela explained that she always got nervous before a gig. Since this was the band's biggest crowd yet, she was the most fearful she had ever been. She could practice for a thousand hours, but when the moment of reckoning arrived, she felt as if she would lose her lunch.

4   Jorge assured her that he knew lots of tricks to conquer stage fright. Pick a friendly, smiling face in the audience, he explained, and keep your eyes on that smile the whole time; play just to that person if you have to.

5   Sela thanked him, but she felt that her <u>trepidation</u> was much bigger than what tricks could fix. Despite playing piano for most of her life, she was beginning to worry that maybe she wasn't destined for performing. In her room, she could take out the keyboard and play perfectly for hours. She could hum a new tune, and her hands would gambol across the keys instinctively, the melody teeming, but if her little brother entered the room, her gift vanished like a ghost.

6   Sela listened to Shaz and Zoë, who were harmonizing brilliantly in the wings. Sela asked them how they stayed so composed.

7   Shaz explained that she ignored the audience completely: "I pretend there's a

Go to next page

big wall between us so I can't get to them, and more importantly, they can't get to me." She gave a look that a lion might give a rabbit. Her rationale seemed sensible, but Sela was positive it wouldn't work for her. She already thought of the audience as her adversary, and that wasn't working.

8   "What's the point of performing if there isn't an audience?" Zoë asked. Even Zoë's speaking voice made people swoon because it was distinctive and melodic. Zoë looked fantastic and sounded better, and it was no mystery to Sela that Zoë wasn't the least bit troubled by performing.

9   Zoë's fearlessness terrified Sela; she started to think that perhaps she wasn't meant to be an entertainer. She thought that maybe she was meant to be a music writer who sat at home and played her piano and didn't bother with performing. For her entire life, Sela had fantasized mounting a stage and rocking an audience, but when it mattered most, she lost her nerve.

10   Sela knew the minutes before showtime were disappearing, and she began to tremble. She paced past the fog machine, the manufactured smoke chilly on her damp skin, and Jules walked out from behind a gigantic amplifier. With her drumsticks, she was counting out a beat on the palm of her hand, and she took a break to wipe sweat from her forehead.

11   Sela was about to say that Jules had nothing to be worried about because all Jules had to do was pound out a beat. She could disappear into the back of the stage and hide behind her huge drum kit. She didn't have to stare at those keys swimming together, becoming indistinguishable. Just as Sela was about to go into this diatribe, Jules spoke.

12   "I wish I were more like you," Jules said. "You know, a born performer."

13   Sela looked at Jules peculiarly. What was she talking about?

14   "I mean, sometimes I look at you up there, right at the edge of the stage, playing and singing so magnificently, and I don't know how you do it."

15   Sela contemplated this because she had never imagined that someone felt this way about her. She was constantly in awe of people she thought were good performers, and it was hard to acknowledge that someone perceived her that way.

16   "You know how I deal with my stage fright?" Jules asked in a low and timid voice, and Sela waited for her to continue.

Go to next page

17 "I pretend that I'm you, that I'm confident and self-assured and above all, that I'm really, really talented."

18 The announcer introduced Sela's band and Jules walked past Sela and into the spotlight. Along with the rest of the girls, Sela stepped out in front of the audience, into the applause and the excitement and this new feeling, not like apprehension at all. Instead, Sela felt like the crowd and the song and the band were all one. The audience wasn't a distraction anymore; the crowd was like a chorus or a bridge, just one more part of the music.

20 Shaz's lionlike gaze is designed to show that

   A. she does not want to be seen by the audience.

   B. she intends to pounce on the audience.

   C. she will not be friendly to the audience.

   D. she is not intimidated by the audience.

21 Which sentence explains Sela's worries?

   A. She is scared that she will forget the words to her songs.

   B. She is afraid that she is not meant to be a performer.

   C. She is afraid that she has not practiced enough.

   D. She is scared that the audience will laugh at her.

22 Why does Jules tell Sela that she wishes she were more like her?

   A. to soothe Sela's nerves about performing

   B. to tell Sela her own fears about performing

   C. to prevent Sela from quitting the band

   D. to get Sela to tell Jules that she is good

23 In paragraph 5, Sela thanks Jorge for his advice, but "felt that her trepidation was much bigger than what tricks could fix."

Which definition represents the intended meaning of the word trepidation?

   A. shyness

   B. joy

   C. anxiety

   D. astonishment

Go to next page

24 Which idea from the story is an example of irony?

    A.   Shaz and Zoë rehearsing their songs in the hallway

    B.   Jules pretending to be Sela to overcome her stage fright

    C.   Jorge advising Sela to pick out a friendly face in the audience

    D.   Zoë explaining that the point of performing is to please the audience

25 In the space provided, summarize the last paragraph of the passage. (2 points)

26 In paragraph 5, the writer uses the phrase "vanished like a ghost" to describe Sela's gift because

    A.   she forgets the notes when her little brother is hovering around her.

    B.   she suddenly loses the confidence to play when others are listening.

    C.   she wishes she could look right through everyone while she is playing.

    D.   she unwillingly plays even though she knows her skills are thin and frail.

27 Which statement characterizes Sela's attitude toward her fellow band members?

    A.   Sela admires the other girls for performing well without fear.

    B.   Sela resents the other girls for being able to sing so melodically.

    C.   Sela envies the other girls for looking fantastic on stage.

    D.   Sela praises the other girls for overshadowing her performances.

Go to next page

Excerpt from "Is It a Crime for a Citizen of the United States to Vote?"

by Susan B. Anthony

Before the Nineteenth Amendment was passed in 1920, civil rights leader Susan B. Anthony shocked people by daring to vote in the 1872 presidential election. Several days later, she was arrested and charged with illegal voting. Anthony pleaded not guilty to the charge and then traveled around the country, campaigning for women's right to vote.

1   Friends and Fellow-citizens: I stand before you to-night, under indictment for the alleged crime of having voted at the last Presidential election, without having a lawful right to vote. It shall be my work this evening to prove to you that in thus voting, I not only committed no crime, but, instead, simply exercised my citizen's right, guaranteed to me and all United States citizens by the National Constitution, beyond the power of any State to deny.

Go to next page

2   Our democratic-republican government is based on the idea of the natural right of every individual member thereof to a voice and a vote in making and executing the laws. . . . The Declaration of Independence, the United States Constitution, the constitutions of the several states and the <u>organic</u> laws of the territories, all alike propose to protect the people in the exercise of their . . . rights. . . .

3   . . . One-half of the people of this nation to-day are utterly powerless to blot from the statute books an unjust law, or to write there a new and a just one. The women, dissatisfied as they are with this form of government, that enforces taxation without representation, —that compels them to obey laws to which they have never given their consent, —that imprisons and hangs them without a trial by a jury of their peers, that robs them, in marriage, of the custody of their own persons, wages and children, —are this half of the people left wholly at the mercy of the other half, in direct violation of the spirit and letter of the declarations of the framers of this government, every one of which was based on the immutable principle of equal rights to all. . . .

4   The preamble of the federal constitution says:

5   "We, the people of the United States, in order to form a more perfect union, establish justice, insure domestic tranquility, provide for the common defense, promote the general welfare and secure the blessings of liberty to ourselves and our posterity, do ordain and established this constitution for the United States of America."

6   It was we, the people, not we, the white male citizens, nor yet we, the male citizens; but we, the whole people, who formed this Union. And we formed it, not to give the blessings or liberty, but to secure them; not to the half of ourselves and the half of our posterity, but to the whole people—women as well as men. And it is downright mockery to talk to women of their enjoyment of the blessings of liberty while they are denied the use of the only means of securing them provided by this democratic-republican government—the ballot.

Go to next page

28 The phrase "framers of this government" (paragraph 3) is used to mean

    A.   those who are allowed to vote.

    B.   those who prevent women from voting.

    C.   those who protect the territories.

    D.   those who created the U.S. Constitution.

29 "And it is downright mockery to talk to women of their enjoyment of the blessings of liberty while they are denied the use of the only means of securing them provided by this democratic-republican government—the ballot."

Which sentence paraphrases the line given above?

    A.   The government makes fun of women for wanting to vote and become involved in government.

    B.   It is ridiculous to pretend that women have many rights when they cannot vote on the laws that provide those rights.

    C.   Women have been blessed with many freedoms except for the right to vote in presidential elections.

    D.   The government is very secure, which means that women should not have to worry about voting at all.

30 "The Declaration of Independence, the United States Constitution, the constitutions of the several states and the <u>organic</u> laws of the territories, all alike propose to protect the people in the exercise of their . . . rights."

In this excerpt from paragraph 2, the word <u>organic</u> means

    A.   just.

    B.   great.

    C.   basic.

    D.   former.

Go to next page

31 Based on paragraph 3, which of the following is probably true?

A. At this time, all assets of married women were transferred to their husbands upon marriage.

B. At this time, only women who worked and had children were allowed to vote.

C. At this time, women were allowed to influence a small part of the lawmaking process.

D. At this time, only women who contributed their wages to the government were considered individuals.

32 Why does the author contrast the language of the U.S. Constitution to the way the government is actually run in this country?

A. to show that the government has changed the language of the Constitution

B. to establish that government officials do not know what they are doing

C. to prove that the government often acts in opposition to the laws written in the Constitution

D. to show that the Constitution is a very outdated document and that the language needs to be updated

33 According to the passage, what was the original purpose of the U.S. Constitution and the Declaration of Independence? Give an example from the passage that supports your explanation. Write your answer in the space provided. (2 points)

Go to next page

Excerpt from "The Tidings"

by Denis Florence MacCarthy

1 A bright beam came to my window frame,
This sweet May morn,
And it said to the cold, hard glass:
Oh! let me pass,
For I have good news to tell,
The queen of the dewy dell,[1]
The beautiful May is born!

2 Warm with the race, through the open space,
This sweet May morn,
Came a soft wind out of the skies:
And it said to my heart—Arise!
Go forth from the winter's fire,
For the child of thy long desire,
The beautiful May is born!

3 The bright beam glanced and the soft wind danced,
This sweet May morn,
Over my cheek and over my eyes;
And I said with a glad surprise:
Oh! lead me forth, ye blessed twain,[2]
Over the hill and over the plain,
Where the beautiful May is born.

4 Through the open door leaped the beam before
This sweet May morn,
And the soft wind floated along,
Like a poet's song,
Warm from his heart and fresh from his brain;

1. *Dell* = valley
2. *Twain* = two things

And they led me over the mount and plain,
To the beautiful May new-born.

5   My guide so bright and my guide so light,
This sweet May morn,
Led me along o'er the grassy ground,
And I knew by each joyous sight and sound,
The fields so green and the skies so gay,
That heaven and earth kept holiday,
That the beautiful May was born.

6   Out of the sea with their eyes of glee,
This sweet May morn,
Came the blue waves hastily on;
And they murmuring cried—Thou happy one!
Show us, O Earth! thy darling child,
For we heard far out on the ocean wild,
That the beautiful May was born. . . .

7   Under the eaves and through the leaves
This sweet May morn,
The soft wind whispering flew:
And it said to the listening birds—Oh, you,
Sweet <u>choristers</u> of the skies,
Awaken your tenderest lullabies,
For the beautiful May now born.

8   The white cloud flew to the uttermost blue,
This sweet May morn,
It bore, like a gentle carrier-dove,
The blessed news to the realms above;
While its sister coo'd[3] in the midst of the grove,
And within my heart the spirit of love,
That the beautiful May was born!

3. *Coo'd* = made the sound of a dove

Go to next page

34 "And it said to the listening birds—Oh, you, / Sweet <u>choristers</u> of the skies, / Awaken your tenderest lullabies, / For the beautiful May now born."

As used in stanza 7, <u>choristers</u> means

A. ears.

B. breezes.

C. singers.

D. clouds.

35 Why did the speaker of the poem say, "Lead me forth"?

A. because the sun was shining and a breeze blew

B. because two people were standing at the window

C. because he wanted to escape the beam and wind

D. because he was trying to find the newborn queen

36 "Through the open door leaped the beam before / This sweet May morn, / And the soft wind floated along, / Like a poet's song."

Which sentence paraphrases the lines given above?

A. The wind is beautiful.

B. The wind is musical.

C. The wind is sweet smelling.

D. The wind is gentle.

37 What is the intended effect of the description in stanza 6, that from the sea "came the blue waves hastily on"?

A. The waves flowed swiftly out of the sea.

B. The waves flowed angrily out of the sea.

C. The waves flowed serenely out of the sea.

D. The waves flowed briefly out of the sea.

38 "May" can be viewed as a metaphor for the

A. beauty of a spring day.

B. birth of a child.

C. hope of finding love.

D. end of a sorrowful time.

OHIO GRADUATION TESTS

Writing

Practice Test 1

PRACTICE TEST 1: WRITING

The maximum time allowed for the test is 2½ hours. Plan your time to respond completely to the two writing-prompt questions, because they are worth 36 of the 48 total possible points on this test. One writing-prompt question is at the beginning of the test; the other is at the end. You may refer to the questions as often as necessary.

For writing-prompt questions, the Answer Sheet includes space for prewriting activities. Use this section to plan your writing. Nothing you write in this space will be scored.

Make sure you write the draft you want scored in the correct space in the Answer Sheet. Your draft needs to be legible to be scored. You may use printed or cursive handwriting.

Revising and editing are encouraged, although you will not be able to use reference materials for this test. Erasing, crossing out and other editing changes may be made right on your draft. You may not need to use the entire space provided, but be sure your answer is complete.

Most of the multiple-choice questions are associated with brief paragraphs or sentences. Some of the questions are clustered together; others stand alone. After reading the paragraph or sentence and the question, choose the correct answer and mark the corresponding circle in your Answer Sheet. If you change an answer, be sure to erase the first mark completely.

For the short-response question, answer completely in the space provided. You may not have to use the entire space provided, but be sure your answer is complete.

1   Some high schools have considered requiring students to choose a major, much like a major people choose in college, by the time they reach tenth grade. The purpose of such a policy is to get students to think about the future and choose classes that will hold their interest. Before adopting a similar policy, your superintendent has decided to ask students for their opinions.

Write to the superintendent stating your opinion. Persuade him or her to agree with your view. Write your response in the space provided on the following pages.

Go to next page

PREWRITING
Important! Use the space below only to plan and practice your response.

_____

_____

_____

_____

_____

_____

_____

_____

_____

_____

_____

_____

_____

_____

_____

_____

_____

_____

_____

_____

_____

_____

_____

_____

_____

_____

_____

Go to next page

Read the following outline and answer question 2.

Outline for Guidebook on Maintaining an Aquarium for Tropical Fish

I. Choosing Tropical Fish

    A. Types of Tropical Fish

        1. Freshwater

        2. Saltwater

    B. Behavioral Considerations

II. Maintaining Water Quality

    A. Filters

    B. Temperature

    C. Cleaning

III. Tropical Fish Food

IV. Signs of Tropical Fish Illnesses

2   In which section of the outline would you find the following sentence?

If you plan to add more fish to your aquarium, you should consider buying a larger filtration system to keep the water clean and healthy.

    A. Section IA

    B. Section IIA

    C. Section IIB

    D. Section IV

Use the following information from a handbook on language to answer question 3.

- Capitalize words such as *history* and *science* only when they refer to the specific titles of courses: She took *History 101*. It was about the *history* of America.

- Capitalize specific periods in history: the *Jurassic Period* of the *Mesozoic Era*.

- Capitalize the names of planets and other heavenly bodies: *Pluto, the Kuiper Belt*.

3 Which is the correct way to edit the sentence below?

We learned in astronomy II that Galileo, who lived during the Renaissance in Italy, discovered the four satellites of Jupiter after building his own telescope.

A. We learned in astronomy II that Galileo, who lived during the Renaissance in Italy, discovered the four Satellites of Jupiter after building his own telescope.

B. We learned in Astronomy II that Galileo, who lived during the renaissance in Italy, discovered the four satellites of Jupiter after building his own telescope.

C. We learned in Astronomy II that Galileo, who lived during the Renaissance in Italy, discovered the four satellites of Jupiter after building his own telescope.

D. We learned in Astronomy II that Galileo, who lived during the Renaissance in Italy, discovered the four satellites of jupiter after building his own telescope.

Go to next page

Use the following information from a handbook on language to answer question 4.

- Use a semicolon to join two or more independent or main clauses that are not connected by a coordinating conjunction. Coordinating conjunctions are *and, but, or, nor, for, so* and *yet.*

- Use a semicolon before a conjunctive adverb when the word connects two independent or main clauses in a compound sentence. Conjunctive adverbs include *however, in addition, instead, for example* and *therefore.*

4   Which of these sentences should be edited to correct an error?

A.   Sharon went to her grandmother's ninetieth birthday party; it was on Saturday.

B.   Her grandmother enjoyed the polka music played by the band, and she even danced a few times.

C.   Sharon's whole family sang to her grandmother and gave her presents; in addition, they took a picture of her with all her grandchildren.

D.   Her grandmother was tired at the end of the day, therefore, she finished her birthday by going to bed early.

5   Select the correct way to edit the following sentence.

In my biology class last week, we studied the structure of plant cells constructed models of plant cells and viewing plant cells under a microscope.

A.   In my biology class last week we studied the structure of plant cells constructed models of plant cells and viewed plant cells under a microscope.

B.   In my biology class last week we studied the structure of plant cells, constructed models of plant cells and viewing plant cells under a microscope.

C.   In my biology class last week, we studied the structure of plant cells, constructed models of plant cells and viewed plant cells under a microscope.

D.   In my biology class last week, we studied the structure of plant cells; constructed models of plant cells and viewed plant cells under a microscope.

6   Officials in your school are concerned that high school students are not making valuable contributions to their community through volunteer work. The officials are considering making community service a requirement for graduation.

You are planning a letter to your principal either supporting or opposing community service as a graduation requirement. Identify two arguments you would use to support or oppose the community service requirement. Write your response on the lines below.

Go to next page

Read the draft paragraph and answer question 7.

¹ I love nature, so it only makes sense that my favorite summer activity is spending time at our cabin on the lake. **²** The cabin, which sits in a clearing among the trees, has a balcony that overlooks the water and a dock situated at the lake's edge. **³** In the mornings, my father and I get up early to go fishing; in the afternoons, we return home with our catch and grill it for dinner. **⁴** After dinner, we build a big fire, wrap ourselves in warm blankets and tell ghost stories until bedtime.

7 Where should the sentence below be inserted into the paragraph?

My mother usually supplies foil-wrapped potatoes and vegetables, too.

A. after sentence 1
    I love nature, so it only makes sense that my favorite summer activity is spending time at our cabin on the lake. **My mother usually supplies foil-wrapped potatoes and vegetables, too.** The cabin, which sits in a clearing among the trees, has a balcony that overlooks the water and a dock situated at the lake's edge. . . .

B. after sentence 2
    . . . The cabin, which sits in a clearing among the trees, has a balcony that overlooks the water and a dock situated at the lake's edge. **My mother usually supplies foil-wrapped potatoes and vegetables, too.** In the mornings, my father and I get up early to go fishing; in the afternoons, we return home with our catch and grill it for dinner. . . .

C. after sentence 3
    . . . In the mornings, my father and I get up early to go fishing; in the afternoons, we return home with our catch and grill it for dinner. **My mother usually supplies foil-wrapped potatoes and vegetables, too.** After dinner, we build a big fire, wrap ourselves in warm blankets and tell ghost stories until bedtime.

D. after sentence 4
    . . . After dinner, we build a big fire, wrap ourselves in warm blankets and tell ghost stories until bedtime. **My mother usually supplies foil-wrapped potatoes and vegetables, too.**

Go to next page

Use the following information from a handbook on language to answer question 8.

Use a comma

- to separate three or more words, phrases or clauses in a series: The bowl was filled with *apples, grapes and pears*.

- to separate adjectives that equally modify the same noun: The *cold, damp* cloth felt good on my face.

- to set off introductory words, phrases or clauses from the rest of the sentence: However, there just wasn't enough time.

- to set off parenthetical elements: This ice cream is, *by far*, the best I've ever tasted.

8   Which is the correct way to edit the sentence below?

In an unfortunate turn of events Tyrone tripped and stumbled before reaching the finish line.

A.   In an unfortunate turn of events, Tyrone, tripped and stumbled before reaching the finish line.

B.   In an unfortunate turn of events Tyrone tripped, and stumbled before reaching the finish line.

C.   In an unfortunate turn of events, Tyrone tripped and stumbled, before reaching the finish line.

D.   In an unfortunate turn of events, Tyrone tripped and stumbled before reaching the finish line.

Go to next page

Read the draft paragraph and answer questions 9 through 12.

[1] The city is a magnificent light show at night accompanied by the songs of sirens, horns and excited chatter. [2] During the day, the sidewalks are a melting pot of people from diverse cultures and backgrounds. [3] Theaters, concert halls and stores are found on every corner. [4] Amazing aromas drift from every restaurant in town: Italian, Greek, Chinese, Mexican and more. [5] There is something here to please just about everyone.

9   In the context of the paragraph, which transitional phrase would be appropriate to use at the beginning of sentence 5?

A.   After a while, there is something here to please just about everyone.

B.   In other words, there is something here to please just about everyone.

C.   Otherwise, there is something here to please just about everyone.

D.   Likewise, there is something here to please just about everyone.

10   In the context of the paragraph, which is the correct way to revise and/or edit sentence 1 for clarity?

A.   At night, the city is a magnificent light show accompanied by the songs of sirens, horns and excited chatter.

B.   The city is, at night, a magnificent light show accompanied by the songs of sirens, horns and excited chatter.

C.   The city is a magnificent light show accompanied by the songs of sirens, horns and excited chatter at night.

D.   The city is a magnificent light show accompanied by the songs of sirens at night, horns and excited chatter.

Go to next page

11 Which topic sentence would be appropriate for the paragraph?

    A.   The city is a crowded, noisy place to live.

    B.   If you like excitement, the city is the place to be.

    C.   I wonder what it would be like to live outside the city.

    D.   The city can be dangerous if you don't know your way around.

12 If the writer chooses to revise and expand the paragraph, which strategy would be appropriate?

    A.   include some information about museums in the city

    B.   include details about smog and traffic congestion

    C.   include some information about job opportunities in the city

    D.   include details about the city's history and growth

13 Think about a moment in time when you felt proud of yourself. Maybe you led your football team to a victory or made the honor roll at school. Explain why this moment made you feel so proud. Be sure to support your essay with specific examples and details. Write your response in the space provided on the following pages.

Go to next page

PREWRITING
Important! Use the space below only to plan and practice your response.

_____

_____

_____

_____

_____

_____

_____

_____

_____

_____

_____

_____

_____

_____

_____

_____

_____

_____

_____

_____

_____

_____

_____

_____

ANSWERS AND EXPLANATIONS
PRACTICE TEST 1: READING

1 **Sample answer**   Reading Process B: Informational, Technical and Persuasive Text D

William Randolph Hearst made the *Journal* as popular as the *World* by presenting the news as entertainment rather than hard news. The headlines in the *Journal* were more enticing and interesting than those in most newspapers, and the writing of the stories was suspenseful. Reading the *Journal* was more like reading a fiction story than a serious news story, which was different from how most papers presented the news.

Another way the *Journal* was not like most newspapers was that it appealed to people outside the society that most newspapers attracted—for instance, women and poor people. The *Journal* appealed to them by lowering its price and presenting stories that those types of people would be interested in. In this way, the *Journal* was different from most newspapers of the day.

Finally, during the Cuban Revolution, the *Journal* printed stories that clearly favored the side of the revolutionaries. It presented the issue more like a soap opera than a national event, which many readers enjoyed. However, this is not how most newspapers write stories. Most journalists remain objective throughout articles.

2   C   Acquisition of Vocabulary A

Some of the stories in the *Journal* were not true; they were fictional.

3   B   Acquisition of Vocabulary A

New York newspapers termed Hearst and Pulitzer's reporting style "yellow journalism."

4   A   Reading Process A

Paragraphs 3 and 4 discuss how Hearst took on failing newspapers, the *San Francisco Examiner* and the *New York Journal*, and molded them into two of the most successful newspapers in the country.

5   B   Reading Applications: Informational, Technical and Persuasive Text B

Yellow journalism is a type of reporting based on deception. It is ironic that the founder of this underhanded practice lent his name to one of the most prestigious awards worldwide.

6 D Reading Applications: Informational, Technical and Persuasive Text D

This is not a fictional account, so it is not meant to entertain. It is also not a persuasive piece. It is informative. The passage was written to inform readers about the topic and events discussed in the passage.

7 C Reading Process B

According to the passage, people enjoyed the new, exciting style of the paper, which drew in more types of readers than ever before.

8 B Reading Applications: Informational, Technical and Persuasive Text A

This quote compares the newspapers that embraced yellow journalism, which took into account the ideas and opinions of minority readers, with the more standard newspapers.

9 D Acquisition of Vocabulary C

When Hearst's illustrator told him that there was no war on which to report, Hearst suggested that he draw pictures of war as if a war were actually occurring, and that he would fabricate a story to go with the pictures.

10 Sample answer Reading Process A

Once Pulitzer helped introduce yellow journalism to the world, other newspapers began to adopt similar formats. One newspaper owner, William Randolph Hearst, who had worked under Pulitzer, copied the format so well that he was able to transform the failing *San Francisco Examiner* into a top-selling paper.

11 C Reading Applications: Literary Text C

The narrator has experienced some horrible things in his life. He seems to be unable to truly express the horrors of what he has seen ("I wish I could commit it to paper the feeling with which I beheld it") because the memories are too hard for him to bear.

12 A Reading Applications: Literary Text A

The narrator expresses unhappiness with his lack of knowledge about himself and his mother. Although the other answer choices may also be true, they are not expressed in this excerpt.

13　C　Reading Process A

The narrator dedicates a paragraph to the recollection of his mother's presence in his home a few times in his life. He explains that she always came at night and was gone by the time he woke up, making his memories of her very vague and unclear.

14　B　Acquisition of Vocabulary A

The word *improper* in this sentence can help you figure out the meaning of *impertinent*. It was improper for a slave to ask questions of his master because it showed a lack of respect for the slave's place within society.

15　**Sample answer**　Reading Applications: Literary Text A

The first memory that appears to disturb the narrator is the fact that he does not know exactly how old he is, and that his master kept him ignorant by withholding that knowledge from him. The second disturbing memory arises when the narrator discusses the Maryland custom of separating slave children from their parents at an early age, and how he barely knew his mother as a result. The third thing that seems to disturb the narrator is the recollection that he did not emotionally acknowledge his mother's death. Looking back, he feels that he should have felt more sorrow and remorse at her death. Finally, the narrator describes the cruel treatment of the slaves by the overseer and master, and how they beat slaves so badly that the narrator still cannot describe how he felt when he witnessed it.

16　A　Reading Applications: Literary Text F

The narrator was kept "in the dark" about his past and his roots. His master would not allow him to ask about his birth; and because the narrator's mother came to him only when he was sleeping, he apparently did not have the opportunity to ask her when he was born. She was a murky figure in his memory, almost as if her presence had been a dream.

17　C　Reading Process B

The narrator says that slave children were separated from their parents as infants, most likely to prevent the child and mother from forming an affectionate bond. During the mother's visits, she does not communicate much with him, but her presence as he falls asleep is the most affection she can show for him.

18 **Sample answer** Reading Applications: Literary Text C

Conflict is the driving force of this story. The narrator is describing some of the conflicts with which he has dealt ever since he was born. He describes his upset at not knowing his age, which results as a conflict between the narrator and his master. He also describes how he and his mother did not communicate much because he only saw her a few times in his life, and always at night. Without these and the other conflicts and hardships described by the narrator, there would not be a story to tell.

19 B Acquisition of Vocabulary A

The narrator considers himself disadvantaged because the white children know their ages but he does not. They have been afforded a privilege that he has been denied, which gives them an advantage over him.

20 D Reading Applications: Literary Text A

Shaz holds this gaze when she talks about imagining a wall between herself and the audience. She wears this facial expression to show that the audience does not intimidate her and that she is able to perform even if they are all watching her.

21 B Reading Applications: Literary Text A

In this story, we learn that Sela believes she might not be destined to be a performer. That is where her anxiety originates.

22 B Reading Process A

When Jules tells Sela that she wishes she were more like her, she is simply expressing her own fears about performing. She was not present when Sela was discussing her stage fright with the other band members. Readers can tell that she is nervous before she speaks to Sela, because she is sweating.

23 C Acquisition of Vocabulary E

Using the context of the sentence and the surrounding paragraphs, you can conclude that Sela is suffering from severe stage fright and is anxious about performing. Therefore, you can determine that *trepidation* and *anxiety* have nearly the same meaning.

24 B Reading Applications: Literary Text A

It is ironic that Jules pretends to be Sela to give herself confidence, because Sela is having a very hard time exhibiting confident behaviors.

25 Sample answer   Reading Process A

Once Sela finds out how Jules feels about her, she is able to boost her own self-confidence. She steps out onto the stage and feels excited rather than nervous. She also learns to view the audience as an essential part of the performance rather than an annoying nuisance.

26 B   Reading Applications: Literary Text F

As soon as someone is listening to Sela play, her confidence vanishes in an instant, leaving her to question whether or not it was there to begin with.

27 A   Reading Applications: Literary Text A

Sela wants to be able to play without fear, and she admires her fellow band members for being able to do so.

28 D   Reading Applications: Informational, Technical and Persuasive Text D

Susan B. Anthony is making the point that when the men who founded our government created the U.S. Constitution, they did not intend for any American citizen to be denied rights.

29 B   Reading Process B

The point here is that the government tells women that they have and benefit from all the freedoms and rights provided by the Constitution, yet women are not allowed to influence or secure these freedoms by voting.

30 C   Acquisition of Vocabulary A

As used in the speech, the word *organic* means *basic*. Anthony uses this word to show that the most fundamental rights are granted to all people, not a select few. This helps support her argument that nowhere in the U.S. Constitution does the language suggest that women should be denied the right to vote.

31 A   Reading Applications: Informational, Technical and Persuasive Text A

Anthony makes the point that after marriage, women of that time were required to give up all of their personal rights, as well as their money and legal custody of their children, to allow their new husbands to control all the assets.

32 C Reading Applications: Informational, Technical and Persuasive Text D

Anthony cites the language of the Constitution to show that the leaders of the country are going against the rules established by their forefathers, and that the forefathers never intended for women to be denied the right to vote.

33 Sample answer Reading Applications: Informational, Technical and Persuasive Text D

The U.S. Constitution and the Declaration of Independence were designed to guarantee citizens certain rights and protect them when they exercise their rights. The founders of the American government based these documents on the principle of equal rights for all citizens, not a select group.

34 C Acquisition of Vocabulary A

Choristers are singers. The speaker is referring to the birds singing in the skies. The word *lullabies* in the following line also offers a clue to the meaning of the word.

35 A Reading Applications: Literary Text A

The speaker is addressing the sun and breeze coming to his window.

36 D Reading Process A

The words *soft* and *floated* offer clues. In addition, the phrase "a poet's song" suggests something that appeals to the soul rather than just the senses.

37 A Acquisition of Vocabulary C

The poet uses the word *hastily* to say that the waves came swiftly from the sea.

38 A Reading Applications: Literary Text F

The poet describes the warm sun, the blue sky and white clouds, the singing birds and the grass, all of which are usually associated with spring.

ANSWERS AND EXPLANATIONS
PRACTICE TEST 1: WRITING

1   **Sample answer**   Writing Applications / Writing Conventions E

Dear Superintendent Juarez:

It is my opinion that requiring students to choose a major by the tenth grade is an excellent idea, and I have two main reasons for feeling this way. First, by the time most students reach tenth grade, they have some idea of which career path they would like to follow. They are starting to look around at colleges or jobs that will put them on the right track to reach their goals. They compare to see which colleges have the best English or art or science programs. They check the papers for job opportunities in the areas where they want to live. It seems only natural that they take courses in school that will help them get a better feel for the careers they plan to pursue. It is better to find out sooner, rather than later, that a career choice is right or wrong. Why should students wait until college, when they are paying hundreds or even thousands of dollars for each credit or course, to find out that they don't really want to be journalists or teachers or doctors?

Another reason I am in favor of choosing a major in tenth grade is that it will give students a chance to tailor their educations to their special interests. If a student is a great musician, plans to study music in college and hopes to one day play in an orchestra, why should that student have to take Advanced Physics? It would make more sense for that student to concentrate on music classes that could help him or her enter a college with an excellent music program. Likewise, if a student is planning to become an auto mechanic, he or she could take classes in auto repair to prepare for that career.

A tailored education not only would help students in the future but also would help them stay focused on their studies in the present. Students would be more likely to pay attention in classes that focus on material they find interesting than in classes full of material they find boring. If given this opportunity, students might even begin to earn better grades. Adopting a system that enables students to choose the education that is right for them could even lead to a decrease in the number of students who drop out before graduation.

Sincerely,

Michelle Marsella

2   B   Writing Processes B

The section of the outline about filters is most likely where you would find information about the best filtration system to accommodate a large number of fish in an aquarium.

3   C   Writing Processes E

This is the only sentence that applies correct capitalization rules to the title of a course, a period in history and the name of a planet.

4   D   Writing Processes E

According to the handbook, a semicolon should be used before a conjunctive adverb (in this case, the word *therefore*) when the word connects two independent clauses.

5   C   Writing Processes D

This is the only sentence that correctly uses commas, placing one after the introductory phrase "in my biology class last week" and after the first of three phrases in a series, viz., "studied the structure of plant cells, constructed models of plant cells and view plant cells under a microscope."

6   **Sample answer**   Writing Processes A

I think requiring students to perform community service to graduate is a good idea because it gives students a chance to see what a big difference they can make in their communities. Many people do not realize that by spending just a few hours picking up litter on the side of the street, they are making an impact on people's lives and on the environment.

Another reason I think requiring community service to graduate is a good idea is that it teaches students about responsibility and understanding the consequences of their actions. For example, some students in my school think that it is fun to vandalize public property. If those students were made to clean up graffiti at the park, they would begin to realize how hard it is to maintain the beauty of the community and might think twice about vandalizing again.

7   C   Writing Processes C

Sentence 3 is about the narrator and his father catching fish and grilling it for dinner. Since the sentence to be inserted also talks about food, the best place for it is after sentence 3.

8   D   Writing Processes E

"In an unfortunate turn of events" is an introductory phrase and should therefore be followed by a comma. This is the only place in the sentence where a comma should appear.

9   B   Writing Processes C

Sentence 3 lists some of the many activities that people can do in the city. Sentence 4 lists the wide variety of restaurants to demonstrate the many cultures that live together in the city. The best transition to use in sentence 5 is "In other words," because it is restating that the city can accommodate just about anyone and anything.

10   A   Writing Processes C

Since sentence 2 begins with the phrase "During the day," it would make sense for sentence 1 to begin with the phrase "At night." In addition, this phrases makes the sentence sound and flow better than the other answer choices.

11   B   Writing Processes A

The passage talks mostly about positive aspects of the city: the diverse cultures, the magnificent lights, the many places to go and the great foods to eat. Therefore, answer choices A and D do not fit with the tone of the paragraph. Likewise, answer choice C is about possibly leaving the city. Answer choice B is the best choice.

12   A   Writing Processes C

Most of the paragraph is about the excitement and entertainment in the city: beautiful lights, sounds of sirens and horns, theaters, stores and restaurants. Therefore, information about the different types of museums in the city would make the most sense within the context of the paragraph.

13   **Sample answer**   Writing Applications / Writing Conventions C

When I was about four years old, I wanted nothing more than to learn to tie my shoes. I remember watching intently as adults and older children all around me quickly and easily molded their trailing laces into perfect bows. I remember trying to imitate the movements of their hands. However, no matter how hard I tried, my laces remained untied until I could get my mother or father to help me.

One day, while my mother was busy cleaning in another room, I took it upon myself to learn to tie my shoes. I sat down in the middle of the floor and pulled one knee close to my chest. Slipping an old red sneaker onto my foot, I grabbed a shoelace in each hand.

First, I tried twisting the laces together. They quickly unraveled. Next, I tied them into a tight knot, but that didn't work either. I later had to ask my father to remove it for me. Then, suddenly, I had an idea. I grabbed one of my mother's sneakers on which the laces were still tied. I examined the bow for a while. I pulled on one lace and watched as the bow came undone. I pulled the laces apart. Then, like a puzzle, I put the pieces back together. I crossed the laces, and slipped one lace through the hole. I made one loop, and then another. I pulled them tight. It was a perfect bow.

Using my newfound knowledge, I tied my own shoe. I was so proud of myself. I immediately ran to show my mother my new trick. Looking back, I realize now that I was not as proud of tying my shoe as I was proud that I had taught myself to tie my shoe. It was just one tiny step toward becoming the independent person I am today.

OHIO GRADUATION TESTS

Reading

Practice Test 2

PRACTICE TEST 2: READING

Each passage in this test is followed by several questions. After reading the passage, choose the correct answer for each multiple-choice question, and then mark the corresponding circle in the Answer Sheet. If you change an answer, be sure to erase the first mark completely.

For each written-response question, answer completely in the space provided. You may not need to use the entire space.

You may refer to the passages as often as necessary. Make sure the number of the question in this book corresponds to the number on the Answer Sheet. Be sure all your answers are complete.

Logan's Lesson

1   Logan slammed the passenger door of his father's pickup truck and gazed warily at the main entrance of the Lakeside Nursing Home. He groaned inwardly and trudged toward the door, each step feeling heavier than the previous one.

2   Inside, Logan was greeted by a receptionist with a smile the size of the Till Plains and more perkiness in her greeting than Logan had been able to muster in his entire life. Her name tag said Suzanne. "You must be Logan," she chirped. "I can't wait for you to meet our residents."

3   Suzanne motioned for Logan to follow her, and he struggled to maintain the Olympic pace she set as she sped down a long corridor toward a set of double doors. A sign near the doors indicated that he was standing outside the Recreation Room. Peering through the window, Logan spied about a dozen silver-haired men and women in the room. Two men played a game of checkers in the corner, while another maneuvered a small scooter toward a rack of magazines. A few women sat in a circle of rocking chairs around a television watching a news program. One of them held yarn and knitting needles in her lap. On the far side of the room, one elderly man with white hair sat at a table by himself carving something from a small scrap of wood.

4   "That's Hector. I think you two will get along quite nicely," said Suzanne, pointing to the man at the far table.

5   Suzanne's pager began to beep, and after glancing at the numbers, she sprinted down the corridor. "I'm afraid you're on your own, Logan. I've got to get back to the reception area," she explained as she disappeared around the corner.

6   Logan sighed, shifted his backpack to his left shoulder and shuffled toward Hector's table. As Logan extended his hand to introduce himself, Hector spoke. "Troublemaker, eh?"

7   Logan stepped back and withdrew his hand, the puzzled look on his face prompting Hector to continue.

8   "They always send me the troublemakers," he said, turning back to his wooden sculpture. "That, and your black eye gave you away."

9   Logan raised his hand to touch the painful bruise near his right eye. Hector's insights were correct. Logan's punishment for getting into a fight at school was to spend at least one hour every day at the nursing home until the end of the semester. Mr. Weatherby, the principal at Logan's high school, thought that spending time with some of the elderly residents at Lakeside would help him learn to care about others' thoughts and feelings.

10   Logan settled into the chair across from Hector. He watched silently as sawdust and shavings fell from the scrap of wood in Hector's wrinkled hands, until finally Hector set down his carving knife and placed the finished sculpture on the table. Logan carefully examined the petite form, amazed by the <u>intricate</u> details etched into the wood. It was a boxer wearing a helmet and boxing gloves, his feet slightly separated and his arms in a position indicating that he was ready to fight.

11   Logan glanced at Hector. "A fighter for a fighter," said the old man. With that, he lifted himself from his chair and moved toward the door.

12   "Wait," said Logan. "Aren't we supposed to talk or something?"

13   Hector turned around and winked, then disappeared through the double doors. Glancing at his watch, Logan realized that an hour had already passed and that his father would be waiting for him. He scooped the wooden figurine off the table, wrapped it in a tissue, and placed it in the zippered pouch of his backpack.

Go to next page

14 Logan remained quiet on the way home, thinking about the unusual events of the afternoon. Hector had called him a troublemaker and a fighter. It was a fitting description, but Logan had never intended to be either. It just seemed that sometimes, when someone or something made him angry or upset, he felt the need to release his anger, and the easiest way to do that was to punch, kick, or break something.

15 That night, Logan rummaged through his backpack until he found the boxer statue. Placing it on his desk, he stared at it for a long time. When he finally crawled into bed, he knew what he could discuss with Hector.

16 The next day, Logan looked for Hector in the Recreation Room, but he was nowhere to be found. Returning to the reception area, Logan asked Suzanne for directions to Hector's living quarters, but she informed him that Hector was on the balcony outside the craft room on the second floor. At the top of the steps, Logan made a left as Suzanne had instructed and walked the length of a blue hallway. He opened a door on the left and entered a room lined with shelves and overflowing with cans of paint, bottles of glue, stacks of paper and a mishmash of other art supplies. Through the sliding door, Logan could see Hector standing at an easel, and beyond him, a magnificent view of Lake Erie.

17 "You paint, too," said Logan as he stepped outside.

18 Hector turned toward Logan, revealing a painting so similar to the lakeside view Logan had just admired that the boy wondered if he was looking through an empty frame.

19 "What else do you do?" Logan asked.

20 Hector thought for a moment, and then explained that his numerous creative activities corresponded to how he felt at a particular point in time. When feeling happy or peaceful, he painted, and when feeling lonely or sad, he wrote poetry. When nervous, such as when he's about to meet someone new, he liked to whittle away at a piece of wood. Logan smiled, thinking of the wooden boxer. He was amazed by Hector's artistic abilities—poetry, paintings, drawings, sculptures and carvings—each chosen to convey a certain mood, thought or feeling.

21 "What do you do when you're angry?" asked Logan.

Go to next page

22   This time it was Hector who smiled. "I build things. Whether it's a chair, a table or a simple puzzle, building things helps me release my anger constructively, rather than destructively," he explained.

23   Hector went inside to rinse his paintbrushes, and Logan contemplated what the old man had told him. A few minutes later, Logan joined Hector at the sink. "How do you release your emotions if you have no artistic abilities?" he asked. Like the day before, Hector winked and left Logan standing alone, filled with questions.

24   When Logan arrived home, his mother yelled at him for forgetting to take the trash out. Later, his father grounded him because of Logan's poor showing on his history exam. Retiring to his room for the night, Logan then noticed that his sister's hamster had chewed a hole through one of his new sneakers. Logan could feel his anger building, but just as he was about to explode, he caught a glimpse of the wooden figurine on his desk.

25   Taking a deep breath, Logan thought of Hector. Do something constructive, not destructive, he said to himself. Looking around his room, Logan spied his guitar in the corner. He hadn't touched it in years, but something inside told him to pick it up and play. Sitting on the corner of his bed, he rested the guitar on his lap and began plucking the strings. Instantly, the storm that had been building inside him dissipated, and his shoulders relaxed.

26   Logan played cards with Hector in the Recreation Room the next day, and they exchanged stories about their families and friends. At the end of the hour, Logan hoisted his backpack and guitar case onto his shoulders, said goodbye and started to walk away. When he reached the door, he turned around and winked at Hector.

27   "Thanks," he said.

1   Which sentence explains why Logan is at the Lakeside Nursing Home?

    A.   He is being punished for fighting.

    B.   He wants to learn to make statues.

    C.   He is visiting an old friend.

    D.   His mother thinks it is a good idea.

Go to next page

2 Which might be an appropriate subtitle for the story?

   A. A Cruel School

   B. Not Enough Time

   C. A New Behavior

   D. Wild Smiles

3 Why does Logan wink at Hector at the end of the story?

   A. He has shared a secret with Hector.

   B. He is trying to make Hector laugh.

   C. Hector usually winks at him.

   D. Hector is trying to be constructive.

4 Which statement explains phrase "the storm that had been building inside him dissipated"? (paragraph 25)

   A. Logan's guitar playing is better than Hector's painting.

   B. Logan found it very easy to play the guitar again.

   C. Logan is different from Hector in many ways.

   D. Logan's will to beat his anger stops it from growing.

5 Explain why Hector made a wooden boxer figurine for Logan. Support your explanation by providing an example or detail from the passage. Write your answer in the space provided.

Go to next page

6   "Logan carefully examined the petite form, amazed by the <u>intricate</u> details etched into the wood." (paragraph 10)

Which word represents the meaning of <u>intricate</u>?

A.   pleasant

B.   elaborate

C.   random

D.   primitive

7   What accounts for Logan's uneasiness at the beginning of the story?

A.   He has had an unpleasant experience in a nursing home.

B.   He does not know what to expect at the nursing home.

C.   He does not want to paint pictures in the nursing home.

D.   He has been fighting with his father about the nursing home.

8   Explain the importance of conflict to the development of the story. Give three examples or pieces of information from the story to support your explanation. Write your answer in the space provided. (4 points)

9   In paragraph 16, the word <u>mishmash</u> is used to describe

A.   a puddle of craft glue

B.   a sloppy painting

C.   a jumble of materials

D.   an empty frame

10   Which statement characterizes Hector's attitude toward Logan?

A.   He is happy to help Logan with his problem.

B.   He is amused by Logan's witty jokes.

C.   He is frustrated by Logan's anger.

D.   He is upset because he misses his grandson.

Go to next page

Written in the Stars

1   At some point, you have probably flipped through a magazine or newspaper, looking for your horoscope. Most horoscopes use the month and day of an individual's birth to predict future events in that person's life. Many horoscope columns offer readers warnings as well as advice on love, friendship and career opportunities. Although many people dismiss horoscopes as mindless entertainment, some truly believe in the power of their predictions. These people are not alone. Horoscopes are a part of astrology, an ancient practice that has been a part of history for thousands of years.

2   Once accepted as a science, astrology is the divination of the influences that celestial bodies have on human affairs. More simply, astrology is the belief that our everyday lives are affected by the alignments of the stars, sun, moon and planets. Astrologers believe that they can "see" the future by reading the signs in the heavens. Using a complex system of numbers that includes dates and times, an astrologer can create charts that predict upcoming events. Though some might argue that these charts are created to tell people what they want to hear, astrologers have been using this system for centuries to foretell the future.

3   Astrology is an ancient practice that has existed since the beginning of recorded history. No one is certain where astrology began, though many scholars believe that its origins can be traced to the ancient civilization of Mesopotamia. The ancient Egyptians, Greeks and Chinese practiced astrology. During the early years of these civilizations, people looked to the sky for omens of war, famine, prosperity, and peace. Even some great rulers were known to consult the stars before making strategic political or military decisions.

4   For thousands of years, many people considered astrology to be a branch of astronomy, the scientific study of celestial bodies. Interest in creating more-accurate astrological charts actually led to some important advances in astronomy. It was not

Go to next page

until the seventeenth century that the two practices were separated. During that time, astrological charts were found to be <u>vague</u> and often unreliable, while astronomical studies yielded results that could be scientifically proven. Eventually, astronomy was deemed a "true" science, but astrology was viewed as a form of entertainment. Nevertheless, astrology continues to be practiced by people all over the world. Dozens of astrological traditions are used in various countries. Each tradition interprets certain celestial movements in a different way. However, the one thing that they all have in common is that they believe the positions of heavenly bodies, including stars, meteors and moons, have an effect on the world around us.

LEO

5   The most well known form of astrology is horoscopic astrology. This type of astrology is the form used by astrologers who write the horoscope columns in newspapers and magazines. Horoscopic astrology uses astrological charts to interpret the positions of stars and planets at a specific time to give individual readings. Based on the date and time of a person's birth, he or she is assigned a specific astrological sign. That sign is thought to provide insight into the person's personality and relationships and predict that individual's destiny. In most horoscopic traditions, there are twelve signs that represent the twelve houses of the zodiac. Each house is ruled by a specific planet. Depending on the alignment of a sign's planet, a person could experience a time of great power or weakness.

6   Chinese astrology is another popular form of this ancient practice. This type of astrology is based on a twelve-year cycle. In the Chinese zodiac, there are twelve corresponding animals for every year of the cycle. Each animal represents specific characteristics that can help explain individual personality traits and offer information about events occurring in the coming year. Also important in Chinese astrology is the principle of yin and yang, which represents the delicate balance of the universe. According this tradition, astrology can inform us of when this balance is upset and what can be done to correct it.

Go to next page

7   Astrology has become a major part of our world's culture. Famous authors like Geoffrey Chaucer and William Shakespeare used aspects of astrology in their works. Even our language has been affected by astrology. For example, the word *influenza* comes from the Italian word for *influence*. Influence was once exclusively an astrological term, meaning the power that the stars had on human affairs. Doctors once believed that disease was caused by an adverse alignment of the stars. It is from this belief that the word *influenza* originated.

8   Despite its contributions to our culture, the validity of astrology is often called into question. Many believe that astrology fails to accurately predict future events. Skeptics view any correct prediction as coincidence rather than proof that astrology is a legitimate study. Still, there is no denying astrology's popularity. Many people have a burning desire to know what's going to happen next. This accounts for the thousands of horoscopes that can be found in newspapers, in magazines and online every day. Despite what scientific experts might believe, astrology continues to fascinate those who truly believe that destiny is written in the stars.

11 The author compares the use of astrology with the use of astronomy to show that both astrology and astronomy

    A.   are considered valid scientific practices.

    B.   study celestial bodies such as stars and planets.

    C.   use the movement of stars and planets to predict the future.

    D.   can offer people insight into their personalities.

12 Which sentence summarizes the purpose of paragraph 3 in the passage?

    A.   It establishes the historical significance of astrology.

    B.   It describes the ancient civilization of Mesopotamia.

    C.   It introduces great rulers who believed in astrology.

    D.   It tells about different forms of horoscopic astrology.

Go to next page

13 Explain how astrology has influenced American English. Give a detail or example from the passage that illustrates how the author tries to connect astrology with change or growth in American English. Write your answer in the space provided. (2 points)

14 According to the passage, why does astrology continue to be popular?

A. Scientists have failed to prove its inaccuracy.

B. Astrology is a form of mindless entertainment.

C. Astrology has had an impact on our culture.

D. People will always be curious about the future.

15 What is the focus of the passage?

A. using astrology to avoid conflict and live in harmony

B. cultural entertainment aspects of astrology

C. societal impacts of astrology throughout history

D. promoting astrology as a real science

16 "During that time, astrological charts were found to be <u>vague</u> and often unreliable, while astronomical studies yielded results that could be scientifically proven." (paragraph 4)

In this excerpt from the passage, the word vague means

A. fuzzy.

B. formless.

C. ambiguous.

D. hazy.

17 The author says that Chinese astrology

A. incorporates the balance of the universe.

B. has influenced the English language.

C. often fails to accurately predict future events.

D. is very popular all over the world.

Go to next page

18 The author explains that despite the existence of skeptics, astrology has become a major part of the world's culture. Explain how astrology has become a significant part of our global culture. Support your explanation with at least three examples or details from the passage. Write your answer in the space provided. (4 points)

19 Based on the article, which is probably true?

   A.   Different astrological traditions interpret the stars differently.

   B.   Astrology was first practiced in the lands of ancient Egypt.

   C.   The movements of meteors are not considered in astrological practices.

   D.   Horoscopic astrology is based on a twelve-year cycle.

Go to next page

A Superstition Mission

by Mark Smith

1   "The exam will be on Monday," announced Mrs. Keenan, the science teacher. "You'll have the entire weekend, so there will be no excuse for forgetting to prepare!"

2   Pete squirmed in his seat, his mind reeling with considerations of all the tasks he'd need to perform before the exam. The exam would cover the first five chapters in their massive textbook—chapters that covered topics ranging from earth science to space exploration. He found the material <u>arduous</u> and knew he'd have to really make an effort to get a decent grade.

3   Mentally reviewing his schedule for the weekend, Pete knew right away he'd need to dedicate most of his time over the next few days to preparing for Mrs. Keenan's test. He was going to start preparing immediately after school, but he remembered that it was Friday the thirteenth. Not wanting to jinx himself, Pete instead <u>resolved</u> to start preparing bright and early on Saturday morning. On Friday night, he placed his textbook at the head of his bed and stacked next to it a pile of science handout sheets.

4   "Here's everything I need to absorb by Monday afternoon," he thought, plopping a pillow on top of it all. "So I'll start by sleeping on it so maybe the information will soak up into my brain."

5   Pete rested his tired head on the pillow. Despite the big lump from all the papers underneath, Pete knew his discomfort was necessary. He didn't want a single thing to go wrong with his preparation routine.

6   Pete woke up at nine o'clock on Saturday, since nine was his lucky number. He'd spent the night dreaming, wading in the deluge of science topics he needed to master by Monday. He realized now more than ever that he

Go to next page

needed some special preparations. For breakfast he ate some cereal with marshmallows shaped like traditional good-luck charms like horseshoes and four-leaf clovers. "This'll fill me up with good luck," he thought as he scanned through the topics of his textbook.

7   Each time he saw a new chapter heading in his book, he thought of an appropriate activity to help him absorb its information. For the chapter on the revolutions of planets, he spun his textbook around nine times—nine was his personal lucky number. Then he spun his chair around, too, for good measure. When he saw information about the winds that blew across Earth, he remembered a good-luck ritual of blowing on his hands.

8   "Maybe that'll help my hands write down the correct answers on Monday," Pete thought hopefully.

9   Again, he slept with the textbook and handouts under his pillow, and all day Sunday he observed every superstitious ritual he could think of. He didn't step on any cracks in the sidewalk, he entered and exited his house through the same door and he kept well away from any roving black cats. Then, on Sunday night, Pete carefully chose his lucky sweatshirt, his lucky socks and his lucky baseball cap. He even accessorized with a lucky charm that his grandmother had given him years ago.

10   Pete swaggered into class, feeling assured that his weekend of preparation would pay off. Mrs. Keenan passed out the exams and Pete grabbed his enthusiastically, gripping his old, chewed-up lucky pencil.

11   The next day, Pete found out that he'd failed the test. He shook his head in amazement. "I did everything I could to prepare," he said. "Who'd have thought I'd forget to read the book?"

Go to next page

20 In describing Pete's sleep on Friday night, the author uses the phrase "He'd spent the night dreaming, wading in the deluge of science topics he needed to master by Monday."

The effect of the phrase is to

A. show that Pete was thinking about the many things he needed to study.

B. imply that Pete was overwhelmed by all that he had to learn for the test.

C. indicate that Pete thought his teacher had assigned too much homework.

D. demonstrate that Pete had a good grasp on many science topics.

21 "Pete squirmed in his seat, his mind reeling with considerations of all the tasks he'd need to perform before the exam." (paragraph 2)

Which sentence paraphrases the one above?

A. Pete was learning the material incredibly fast.

B. Pete was imagining running in a marathon.

C. Pete was thinking of a lot of different things.

D. Pete had already studied and was thinking ahead.

22 "He found the material arduous and knew he'd have to really make an effort to get a decent grade." (paragraph 2)

In this excerpt from the passage, the word arduous means

A. delicate.

B. boring.

C. cunning.

D. difficult.

Go to next page

23 What might be an appropriate subtitle for the story?

    A.   How Not to Study

    B.   The Triumph of Effort

    C.   An Unusual Assignment

    D.   Lucky Day

24 In paragraph 3, the author says Pete "resolved to start preparing." Which word represents the intended meaning of resolved?

    A.   procrastinated

    B.   finished

    C.   decided

    D.   hesitated

25 In paragraph 10, the author uses the phrase "swaggered into class" because Pete felt

    A.   embarrassment.

    B.   confidence.

    C.   nervousness.

    D.   astonishment.

26 What accounts for Pete's not studying as soon as he gets home from hearing about the test?

    A.   nervousness about bad luck

    B.   wanting to get a fresh start

    C.   frustration about learning

    D.   craving time with his friends

27 Explain what Pete may have learned from the events in the story. Give an example from the passage that supports your explanation. Write your answer in the space provided. (2 points)

Go to next page

The Yangtze River

1   The Yangtze River stretches about 6,380 kilometers (3,964 miles) across the middle of China, making it the longest river in Asia and the third-longest river in the entire world. It flows west to east, beginning in a glacier in the western Dangla Mountains and drawing water from many lakes and more than 700 tributaries along the way. It virtually divides the country in half horizontally before emptying into the East China Sea at Shanghai. The Yangtze River is so long that it is known by different names throughout the nine different provinces that it occupies. For instance, it is called the Dangqu River at the point of its origin and the Jinsha River near its center. The Yangtze has a great impact on China and is very important to its people.

2   One reason the Yangtze River is so important is that it serves as a major Chinese shipping route, connecting far western inland China to the country's coast in the east. Almost 800 million tons of various cargoes are shipped across its waters each year, entering and leaving the country through ports in Shanghai. It also <u>facilitates</u> irrigation across the country, watering and nourishing crops such as rice and wheat. Although controlled amounts of water have been beneficial to Chinese lands for many years, the river is a temperamental ally. It has overflowed and flooded China many times in the country's ancient history.

Go to next page

3   Another beneficial aspect of the river is its capacity to produce the hydroelectric power used throughout China. In 1995, construction began on the Three Gorges Dam, which is 600 feet tall, is 1.5 miles long and creates a 400-mile-long reservoir that holds 5 trillion gallons of water. Eventually, the dam's electrical output will be equivalent to that of eighteen nuclear power plants, providing one-ninth of China's citizens with power. The dam is also intended to control some of the flooding problems suffered by those in the riverside towns and cities.

28 According to the author, the Yangtze River brings the greatest advantage to the Chinese people by

   A.   carrying more silt than any other river in the world.

   B.   drawing water from many lakes and tributaries.

   C.   beginning as a glacier in the western Dangla Mountains.

   D.   connecting inland China with eastern coastal trading.

29 What pattern does the author use to organize the ideas in the passage?

   A.   chronological order

   B.   key idea with examples

   C.   spatial order

   D.   problem and solution

30 What is the purpose of the passage?

   A.   to explain why the Yangtze is important

   B.   to describe the future uses of the Yangtze

   C.   to persuade readers to visit the Yangtze

   D.   to show the dangers of the Yangtze's flooding

31 The author uses the image of a "temperamental ally" (paragraph 2) to describe

   A.   the benefits of the Yangtze for the Chinese people.

   B.   the trading network based in the Yangtze region.

   C.   the way the Yangtze both helps and hurts people.

   D.   the connection between the Yangtze and other rivers.

Go to next page

32 "It also <u>facilitates</u> irrigation across the country, watering and nourishing crops such as rice and wheat." (paragraph 2)

In this excerpt from the passage, the word <u>facilitates</u> means

A.   keeps alive.

B.   holds responsible.

C.   makes possible.

D.   travels from.

33 Summarize paragraph 3. Write your answer on the lines below. (2 points)

Go to next page

Buckeye Biography

1   Ohio has many unique characteristics and a long list of accomplishments. The state is famous for its long and storied history, its rivers and wildlife and its contribution of eight presidents to the United States. With all these varied claims to fame, how did Ohio come to be known as the Buckeye State? The answer to that puzzling question lies far back in the story of Ohio.

2   Thousands of years ago, the Native Americans who originally inhabited Ohio became well acquainted with the many forests in the region. The native people relied on Ohio's trees for firewood, food and building supplies. One of the types of trees the Indians preferred produced a nut with a distinctive dotted-circle design that resembled a deer's eye. The Indians named this tree *hetuck*; later occupants translated this word as *eye of the buck*, or *buckeye*.

3   After that, several events occurred that make people of the Ohio territory pay special attention to the buckeye tree. The first pioneers who settled in Ohio engaged in tree-chopping contests; certainly, many buckeye trees fell under their axes. A few generations later, some people began using the term *buckeye* as a nickname for other people. Most notably, Colonel Ebenezer Sproat was called "the Big Buckeye." Sproat was a massive, powerful military officer who participated in the Revolutionary War and helped settle the Ohio town of Marietta. His nickname suggested that his size and strength were comparable to that of a large buckeye tree.

4   The event that ensured the lasting fame of the buckeye tree—and inspired Ohio's famous nickname, the Buckeye State—took place in 1840. In that year, the nation was embroiled in a heated presidential campaign. William Henry Harrison, an Ohio veteran, was attempting to win the nation's top leadership position from the current president, Martin Van Buren.

5   Presidential elections of the 1800s were often brutal affairs. Many opposing candidates would viciously <u>assail</u> one another with name calling, slanderous rumors and crude songs. In 1840, supporters of Martin Van Buren decided to portray Harrison as an unsophisticated, uneducated woodsman. They insisted that he was only qualified to lounge around in a log cabin deep in a forest, contributing nothing to society.

Go to next page

6   Harrison's supporters proved to be craftier than their rivals, however. They decided to take the insults and the negative publicity and use both to their advantage. Supporters of William Henry Harrison began proudly touting him as their "Log-Cabin Candidate" and expressing respect for his humble origins. They showed voters that Harrison was not a wealthy, arrogant man but simply an earnest, hardworking laborer. Harrison went so far as to choose the log cabin as his campaign symbol. He had buttons, posters, medals, and even walking sticks made, each embossed with a picture of a log cabin. The logs in that log cabin were none other than buckeye trunks.

7   When Harrison won the election, the log cabin—along with the buckeye tree—became a powerful symbol of the people of Ohio, the Buckeye State.

34 "His nickname suggested that his size and strength were comparable to that of a large buckeye tree." (paragraph 3)

Which sentence paraphrases the line given above?

A.   He gave himself the "buckeye" nickname to feel bigger and stronger.

B.   The nickname showed that he was as big and strong as a buckeye tree.

C.   Buckeyes are strong, tall trees, as suggested by their nickname.

D.   Nicknames can have a major effect on the person they describe.

35 "Many opposing candidates would viciously assail one another." (paragraph 5)

In this excerpt from the passage, the word assail means

A.   attack.

B.   research.

C.   question.

D.   debate.

Go to next page

36 According to the author, Martin Van Buren's description of Harrison's background was designed to

A. cause the people of Ohio to respect Harrison.

B. represent Harrison as unworthy of election.

C. turn the buckeye tree into a great symbol.

D. help more Ohioans become presidents.

37 Which sentence summarizes the purpose of the question in paragraph 1 of the passage?

A. It suggests that buckeyes must be special to Ohio.

B. It introduces the many notable features of Ohio.

C. It convinces the reader to learn more about Ohio.

D. It clarifies the terms used when dealing with Ohio.

38 Which idea from the passage is an example of irony?

A. Buckeye trees produce nuts that look like animal eyes.

B. Native Americans and early settlers alike used buckeyes.

C. Election campaigns were often brutal in the 1800s.

D. Van Buren's insults helped make Harrison more popular.

Stop

OHIO GRADUATION TESTS

Writing

Practice Test 2

PRACTICE TEST 2: WRITING

The maximum time allowed for the test is 2½ hours. Plan your time to respond completely to the two writing-prompt questions, because they are worth 36 of the 48 total possible points on this test. One writing-prompt question is at the beginning of the test; the other is at the end. You may refer to the questions as often as necessary.

For writing-prompt questions, the Answer Sheet includes space for prewriting activities. Use this section to plan your writing. Nothing you write in this space will be scored.

Make sure you write the draft you want scored in the correct space in the Answer Sheet. Your draft needs to be legible to be scored. You may use printed or cursive handwriting.

Revising and editing are encouraged, although you will not be able to use reference materials for this test. Erasing, crossing out and other editing changes may be made right on your draft. You may not need to use the entire space provided, but be sure your answer is complete.

Most of the multiple-choice questions are associated with brief paragraphs or sentences. Some of the questions are clustered together; others stand alone. After reading the paragraph or sentence and the question, choose the correct answer and mark the corresponding circle in your Answer Sheet. If you change an answer, be sure to erase the first mark completely.

For the short-response question, answer completely in the space provided. You may not have to use the entire space provided, but be sure your answer is complete.

---

1   The mayor of your town has closed the old, damaged pool at your local community center. She has not decided whether it is better to renovate and reopen the swimming pool or to keep it closed. Before making a final decision, she has asked for the townspeople's opinions.

Write to the mayor stating your opinion. Persuade her to agree with your view. Write your response on the lines below.

Go to next page

PREWRITING
Important! Use the space below only to plan and practice your response.

Go to next page

Read the following outline and answer question 2.

Outline for Booklet on Fire Safety

I. Tips for Fire Prevention

II. Types of Fires

    A. Class A: Ordinary Combustibles

    B. Class B: Flammable Liquids

    C. Class C: Electrical Fires

    D. Class D: Combustible Metals

III. Types of Extinguishers

    A. Pressurized Water (PW)

    B. Dry Chemical

    C. Carbon Dioxide (CO_2)

IV. Extinguishing a Fire

2   In which section of the outline would you find the following sentence?

When using a fire extinguisher, remember the PASS system: <u>p</u>ull the pin, <u>a</u>im at the fire, <u>s</u>queeze the handle and <u>s</u>weep from side to side.

    A. Section I

    B. Section IIA

    C. Section IIC

    D. Section IV

Go to next page

Use the following information from a handbook on language to answer question 3.

- Capitalize the first word in a full-sentence quotation: Henry said, "The brakes on the car are squeaky.

- Capitalize the names of organizations, associations and political parties: He plays football for the Cincinnati Bengals and volunteers with the American Cancer Society.

- Do not capitalize the names of seasons of the year: Skiing is a fun winter sport.

3   Which is the correct way to edit the sentence below?

Shawna said, "my little sister will be selling cookies for the Girl Scouts this summer."

A.   Shawna said, "My little sister will be selling cookies for the Girl Scouts this summer."

B.   Shawna said, "My little sister will be selling cookies for the Girl Scouts this Summer."

C.   Shawna said, "my little sister will be selling cookies for the girl scouts this Summer."

D.   Shawna said, "My little sister will be selling cookies for the girl Scouts this summer."

Go to next page

Use the following information from a handbook on language to answer question 4.

- Use a semicolon between main clauses not joined by a coordinating conjunction.

- Main clauses contain a subject and a predicate and do not begin with a subordinating word.

- Subordinating words include *because, although, since, as if, so that* and *after*.

- Coordinating conjunctions are *and, but, or, nor, for, so* and *yet*.

- A semicolon may be used to join two independent main clauses connected by an adverb such as *however, therefore, otherwise* or *nevertheless*. The adverb must be followed by a comma.

4   Which sentence combines the sentences below into one sentence by correctly using a semicolon?

The Rock and Roll Hall of Fame and Museum is in Cleveland, Ohio.

And many rock and roll fans venture there each year.

A.   The Rock and Roll Hall of Fame and Museum is in Cleveland, Ohio; and many rock and roll fans venture there each year.

B.   Each year, many rock and roll fans venture to Cleveland, Ohio; the location of the Rock and Roll Hall of Fame and Museum.

C.   Each year, many rock and roll fans venture to the Rock and Roll Hall of Fame and Museum; which is in Cleveland, Ohio.

D.   The Rock and Roll Hall of Fame and Museum is in Cleveland, Ohio; many rock and roll fans venture there each year.

Go to next page

5   Which revision or edit improves the usage in the sentence below?

   A good writer chooses words that support both the main idea and the purpose of their writing.

   A.   A good writer chooses words that support two things: the main idea and the purpose of their writing.

   B.   Good writers choose words that support both the main idea and the purpose of his or her writing.

   C.   A good writer chooses words that support both the main idea and the purpose of his or her writing.

   D.   Good writers want both the main idea and the purpose of their writing to be supported by the words he or she chooses to use.

6   You have been given the assignment to argue the "pro" side in a debate about adopting school uniforms at your high school. Use the information below to organize and write a brief speech about this topic. Your speech should be in paragraph form.

   Benefits of Wearing School Uniforms

   • Reduces violence against students over clothes and shoes

   • Decreases distractions for students while they are trying to learn

   • Strengthens students' sense of community

   • Makes trespassers more recognizable

   • Creates equality among students

   • Reduces costs

   Write your answer on the lines below.

Go to next page

Read the draft paragraph and answer questions 7 – 9.

[1] I've had the dream of becoming a world-famous singer. [2] For some time now. [3] I do vocal exercises to strengthen my voice, drink tea with honey and lemon to soothe my throat and will practice singing in the shower. [4] However, last week I came to a shocking realization. [5] I recorded my voice on a tape and learned that my attempts at singing are horrible!

7   Where should the sentence below be inserted into the paragraph?

Perhaps I will consider pursuing a different career.

A.   after sentence 2
     . . . For some time now. **Perhaps I will consider pursuing a different career.** I do vocal exercises to strengthen my voice, drink tea with honey and lemon to soothe my throat and will practice singing in the shower. . . .

B.   after sentence 3
     . . . I do vocal exercises to strengthen my voice, drink tea with honey and lemon to soothe my throat and will practice singing in the shower. **Perhaps I will consider pursuing a different career.** However, last week I came to a shocking realization. . . .

C.   after sentence 4
     . . . However, last week I came to a shocking realization. **Perhaps I will consider pursuing a different career.** I recorded my voice on a tape and learned that my attempts at singing are horrible!

D.   after sentence 5
     . . . I recorded my voice on a tape and learned that my attempts at singing are horrible! **Perhaps I will consider pursuing a different career.**

Go to next page

8   In the context of the paragraph, what is the correct way to revise sentence 2 to make it a complete sentence?

   A.   Time for some now.

   B.   Now for some time.

   C.   For some time now, I've been trying to improve.

   D.   For some time now, trying and improving.

9   In the context of the paragraph, which revision improves the parallel structure in sentence 3?

   A.   I do vocal exercises to strengthen my voice, drink tea with honey and lemon to soothe my throat and practice singing in the shower.

   B.   I do vocal exercises to strengthen my voice, drinking tea with honey and lemon to soothe my throat and practiced singing in the shower.

   C.   I was doing vocal exercises to strengthen my voice, drink tea with honey and lemon to soothe my throat and will practice singing in the shower.

   D.   I was doing vocal exercises to strengthen my voice, drinking tea with honey and lemon to soothe my throat and practiced singing in the shower.

Go to next page

Use the following draft paragraph to answer questions 10 through 12.

¹ There are lots of things to see in Ohio. ² You can visit the world's oldest traffic light in Ashville. ³ If you're a fan of picnics, perhaps you would enjoy a stop in Dresden where you can visit the world's largest woven basket. ⁴ You can also visit the world's largest Amish buggy, the world's largest rubber stamp and the world's largest cuckoo clock. ⁵ If you're in the mood for a short trip, drive down McKinley Street, the shortest street in America, in Bellefontaine.

10 Which sentence would be an appropriate replacement for sentence 1?

    A.   Have you ever been to Ohio?

    B.   Ohio is home to many interesting tourist attractions.

    C.   There's much to learn about American history in Ohio.

    D.   Ohio is a great place to live.

11 Which phrase is appropriate to add at the beginning of sentence 2?

    A.   As a result,

    B.   As you can see,

    C.   On the other hand,

    D.   For example,

12 Which sentence appropriately summarizes the ideas in sentence 4?

    A.   Several items deemed "the world's largest" are in Ohio.

    B.   All the tourist attractions in Ohio are enormous.

    C.   Ohio has more "world's largest" items than any other state.

    D.   If you come to Ohio, you can see many interesting sites.

Go to next page

13 What is one book that has been especially meaningful to you? This book could be one that you read in school or one that you read on your own time. Explain why reading this book was important to you. Use specific details to explain and support your reasons. Write your response in the space provided on the following pages.

Go to next page

PREWRITING
Important! Use the space below only to plan and practice your response.

_____

_____

_____

_____

_____

_____

_____

_____

_____

_____

_____

_____

_____

_____

_____

_____

_____

_____

_____

_____

_____

_____

_____

_____

ANSWERS AND EXPLANATIONS
PRACTICE TEST 2: READING

1   A   Reading Applications: Literary Text A

It says in the beginning of the story that Logan must spend one hour every day at the nursing home as a punishment for fighting.

2   C   Reading Process A

When Logan feels himself getting angry, he reminds himself of what Hector told him about releasing anger constructively. Instead of exploding, he picks up his guitar. This shows that he is trying out a new behavior to help himself deal with his anger.

3   C   Reading Applications: Literary Text A

Hector usually gives Logan something to think about and then winks at him. At the end of the story, Logan does the same to Hector.

4   D   Reading Process B

Logan usually lets his anger swell and build until its power overtakes him, but he wills it away this time by focusing on the guitar instead of his anger.

5   **Sample answer**   Reading Applications: Literary Text F

Hector made the wooden boxer for Logan to represent Logan's anger. He wanted Logan to have a visual representation of his anger so that Logan would be able to see it and recognize that it is unnecessary. When Logan gets angry at the end of the passage, he looks at the boxer figurine and decides to calm himself down instead of exploding.

6   B   Acquisition of Vocabulary A

Logan is amazed that the tiny figure has details such as boxing gloves and a helmet. This helps the reader to understand that *intricate* means *elaborate*.

7   B   Reading Applications: Literary Text C

Logan does not know what he is going to see or do at the nursing home. He is wary of the nursing home because he is unsure about what will happen there.

8   **Sample answer**   Reading Applications: Literary Text C

Conflict is very important to this story because it is through conflict that Logan eventually learns his lesson. One conflict in the story is that Logan does not want to go to the nursing home, but his principal and parents have forced him to go so he will learn to care about the thoughts and feelings of others. Another conflict arises when Logan does not know what to talk about with Hector. He solves this conflict that night, when he looks at the wooden figurine that Hector gave him. The most important conflict, which appears toward the end of the story, is that Logan struggles with his anger. Through the wisdom and insight of Hector, as well as his own abilities, Logan overcomes this conflict and ends up learning a valuable lesson.

9   C   Acquisition of Vocabulary A

When Logan enters the craft room, he notices that the shelves are overflowing with art supplies. The word *overflowing* can help readers to determine that the supplies are disorganized and jumbled.

10 A   Reading Applications: Literary Text A

Hector seems happy to help Logan with his problem. He likes Logan and most likely feels good about helping him abandon his violent reactions to develop an artistic form of expression instead.

11 B   Reading Applications: Informational, Technical and Persuasive Text D

Both astrology and astronomy involve studying the stars and planets, though in different ways.

12 A   Reading Process A

This paragraph focuses on astrology's having been practiced since the beginning of recorded history. This fact suggests that astrology is historically significant.

13 **Sample answer** Acquisition of Vocabulary D

According to the passage, doctors once believed that a misalignment of the stars was responsible for a certain type of sickness. They thought that the stars "influenced" the body to contract this disease. The disease came to be known as influenza. Although the word also has Italian origins, we still use *influenza* in American English today.

14 D   Reading Process B

In the final paragraph, the author explains that interest in astrology continues because people will always look for some way to predict the future.

15 C   Reading Applications: Informational, Technical and Persuasive Text D

The author consistently points out that astrology has a long and important history, making this the main focus of the passage.

16 C   Acquisition of Vocabulary A

The word *vague* means *uncertain* or *ambiguous*. Astrology was considered a vague practice because many of the predictions made by astrologers could have several different outcomes depending on their interpretations.

17 A   Reading Applications: Informational, Technical and Persuasive Text D

The author discusses the Chinese astrology principle of yin and yang and how it represents the delicate balance of the universe.

18 **Sample answer**   Reading Applications: Informational, Technical and Persuasive Text D

Astrology is a significant part of our global culture because it has been practiced throughout the world since the beginning of recorded history and continues to be common in modern cultures. Ancient civilizations of the world looked to astrology to predict and explain the occurrence of natural and human-influenced events, such as famine and war, which made it a driving force in these cultures. It appears in the historical literatures of many cultures and has affected different languages throughout the world.

The presence of astrological predictions in numerous newspapers, magazines and websites proves that people in many countries today still depend on astrology to predict the future and either take comfort in or receive warning of events to come. Although not everyone agrees on its validity, astrology has been so prevalent in world cultures throughout time that it has gained an undeniable global importance and significance.

19 A   Reading Applications: Informational, Technical and Persuasive Text B

In the fourth paragraph, the author explains that each astrological tradition interprets celestial movements in a different way.

20 A   Reading Applications: Literary Text F

To be caught in a deluge means to be unable to stay afloat, but Pete is not overwhelmed. Pete was merely thinking of the many things that he needed to study.

21 C   Reading Process A

Pete was thinking a lot of different things. None of the other choices makes sense.

22 D   Acquisition of Vocabulary A

The word *arduous* is a synonym for *difficult*.

23   A   Reading Process A

Pete was not very lucky, but he did show readers how not to study.

24   C   Acquisition of Vocabulary C

Pete decided that he would start studying the next day.

25   B   Reading Applications: Literary Text F

To swagger is to strut with confidence. Pete felt certain that by following all his superstitions, he would get a good grade on his test.

26   A   Reading Applications: Literary Text C

Pete does not start studying right away because it is Friday the thirteenth, and he does not want to jinx himself.

27   **Sample answer**   Reading Process B

In the story, Pete learns that you should not get so caught up in your superstitions that you forget about what is most important. In the story, Pete forgets to study for his test because he is too busy worrying about his superstitions.

28   D   Reading Process B

In the passage, the author writes that the Yangtze River is beneficial largely because it allows trading between people in inland China and people along the coast.

29   B   Reading Applications: Informational, Technical and Persuasive Text A

At the end of the first paragraph, the author states that the Yangtze River is important to China. The following paragraphs provide evidence and examples to supports that statement.

30   A   Reading Applications: Informational, Technical and Persuasive Text B

The author talks about the great impact the river has on the people of China. Some of the impact is positive and some is negative, but it is clear that the river is very important.

31   C   Reading Applications: Informational, Technical and Persuasive Text B

The Yangtze is a "temperamental ally" because it not only helps the people of China in many ways but also hurts them during floods that can be catastrophic.

32 C   Acquisition of Vocabulary A

To facilitate is to make something possible or easy. The river does not keep irrigation alive, but irrigation keeps the crops alive. The river does not hold irrigation responsible for anything, but it is responsible for irrigating the crops. The river travels across the country, but again, this choice does not reflect the meaning of the word *facilitate* as it is used in relation to the river.

33 **Sample answer**   Reading Process A

The Three Gorges Dam, built in 1995, will reduce flooding of the Yangtze River and provide hydroelectric power. This power, equal to that of eighteen nuclear power plants, can bring energy to one-ninth of the people in China.

34 B   Reading Process A

Saying that someone's size and strength are comparable to a tree means that he or she is very strong.

35 A   Acquisition of Vocabulary A

This word means "to attack." In the passage, it says that candidates assailed, or attacked, one another with nasty rumors and insults.

36 B   Reading Process B

Van Buren tried to make Harrison look like a simpleton who lived in a log cabin because he was lazy, unsuccessful and unworthy of election.

37 A   Reading Applications: Informational, Technical and Persuasive Text A

The question in the first paragraph asks why, considering all the things that are special about Ohio, the state is known as the Buckeye State. This suggests there is something special about buckeyes, which the passage goes on to explain.

38 D   Reading Applications: Informational, Technical and Persuasive Text B

Irony involves an action getting an unexpected reaction. Here, Van Buren's insults—intended to turn people against Harrison—actually made people respect Harrison.

ANSWERS AND EXPLANATIONS
PRACTICE TEST 2: WRITING

1 **Sample answer** Writing Applications / Writing Conventions E

Dear Mayor Bennigan:

The community center is valuable to the citizens of this town for many reasons. It provides children with a safe place to go after school. It affords townspeople opportunities for both mental and physical exercise. It acts as a gathering place where community members can interact and socialize. It used to include a swimming pool, which allowed community members to cool off and relax on hot summer days. Since the pool has been closed, many community members, including me, have realized what a valuable asset the pool is to the community. I'm sure you are familiar with the saying "You don't know what you've got 'til it's gone." The people of this town need the pool to be reopened—and soon!

While the community center serves as a central meeting place for the people of this town, the pool attracts the most citizens during the summer months. Without the pool, attendance at the community center has not been nearly as high as it was in the past, and this has created a rift in the communications of our townspeople. Community members now catch up with one another in supermarkets aisles and strip mall parking lots, rather than at the community center's poolside. Many would rather stay in their air-conditioned homes than visit the community center to partake in activities that offer no relief from the heat.

The summer heat is an issue in itself. More than half of the citizens of this town do not own swimming pools. Many also lack air-conditioning in their homes, especially elderly citizens. The pool once allowed these people to cool off and enjoy the summer rather than sweat it out at home. It protected residents from conditions such as sunstroke, heatstroke, heat exhaustion and heat rash. Now citizens without pools or air-conditioning units are susceptible to these heat-related conditions. They do not have the option of cooling down at the community pool. This puts many of our valued citizens at a disadvantage.

As you can see, this community needs its pool to function successfully as a cohesive unit. Therefore, I believe that the pool should be remodeled and reopened. Thank you for your consideration of this issue.

Sincerely,

Greg Maines

2 D Writing Processes B

Although section III contains information about extinguishers, it focuses on the various types of extinguishers. Only section IV is about extinguishing a fire, the topic of this sentence. Answer choice D is correct.

3 A Writing Processes E

This is the only sentence that correctly applies capitalization rules to a full-sentence quotation, the name of an organization and a season of the year.

4 D Writing Processes E

This is the only sentence that correctly uses a semicolon. The semicolon is placed between two main clauses that are not joined by a coordinating conjunction.

5 C Writing Processes D

A pronoun should always agree with its antecedent, or the word for which the pronoun is substituted. In this sentence, *their* is a third person plural possessive pronoun. However, its antecedent (*writer*) is singular. Therefore, a third person singular possessive pronoun should be used. Because a writer can be male or female, it is appropriate to use the phrase "his or her," because *his* and *her* are both third person singular possessive pronouns.

6 **Sample answer** Writing Processes A

Ladies and gentlemen, we've all heard the arguments against school uniforms. Many feel that they erase our individuality and trample freedom of expression. Well, today I'm here to present the positive side of school uniforms. I will begin with the most important benefit: safety. Uniforms will help to lessen violence against students over expensive clothes and shoes. They will also allow teachers and administrators to quickly identify trespassers who do not belong on campus.

However, safety is not the only problem that uniforms will help to correct. With everyone wearing the same thing, there will be fewer distractions to pull students' attention away from learning. Uniforms also create a sense of community, because all students will look like they belong to the same team. This, in turn, will help to create equality among students. Finally, uniforms will help to lower the cost of school clothes, because parents won't have to spend hundreds of dollars to keep up with the latest fashions each year. Thank you.

7   D   Writing Processes C

Because the author of the paragraph has been considering a singing career for a long time, he or she probably would not consider a career change until after learning that his or her singing voice is terrible. This sentence would make the most sense after sentence 5.

8   C   Writing Processes D

Only answer choice C is a complete sentence. All the other answer choices are fragments.

9   A   Writing Processes D

Only answer choice A improves the parallel structure of the sentence. Present tense verbs in active voice are used consistently throughout the sentence.

10   B   Writing Processes C

Using the phrase "many interesting tourist attractions" is a more precise way of saying "lots of things to see." This sentence gives readers a clear idea of what the topic of the paragraph is going to be.

11   D   Writing Processes C

Because this sentence gives an example of one of the many tourist attractions in Ohio, using the introductory phrase "For example" is the best choice here.

12   A   Writing Processes C

Answer choices B and C have nothing to do with the information presented in sentence 4. Answer choice D could be considered another candidate for the topic sentence of the whole paragraph, not a summary of sentence 4. Answer choice A is correct.

13   **Sample answer**   Writing Applications / Writing Conventions C

One book that has had an impact on my life is *Treasure Island*, by Robert Louis Stevenson. This book is like nothing else I have ever read. It is the story of a boy, Jim Hawkins, whose parents operate an inn. One day a sea captain dies in the inn, and Jim and his mother realize that pirates might be to blame. Jim finds secret documents among the captain's possessions, including a map to a huge treasure trove. The rest of the book describes Jim's adventures in searching for the treasure and dealing with nasty, yet amazing, pirates.

I read this book two years ago, and it made me look at the world differently. At the time, I was very uncertain about my future. The things I was doing felt dull and repetitive, and I was afraid my life might be the same way. After reading this book, I started to realize that the world is full of excitement—though sometimes it can be very hard to find!

Treasure Island is all about adventure. Of course, life has many serious responsibilities, like work and school, and I know they are important. However, I also believe that everyone should make time to have exciting experiences in which they learn new things and meet new people. I don't want to do the same thing every day. Like Jim, I want to find some adventure in life (but without the pirates!). Jim's great adventures help shape him into a brave and knowledgeable person, like the person I hope to become.

PRACTICE TEST 1: READING

1 _____

_____

_____

_____

_____

_____

_____

_____

2 Ⓐ Ⓑ Ⓒ Ⓓ   **3** Ⓐ Ⓑ Ⓒ Ⓓ   **4** Ⓐ Ⓑ Ⓒ Ⓓ

5 Ⓐ Ⓑ Ⓒ Ⓓ   **6** Ⓐ Ⓑ Ⓒ Ⓓ   **7** Ⓐ Ⓑ Ⓒ Ⓓ

8 Ⓐ Ⓑ Ⓒ Ⓓ   **9** Ⓐ Ⓑ Ⓒ Ⓓ

10 _____

_____

_____

_____

_____

_____

_____

_____

11 Ⓐ Ⓑ Ⓒ Ⓓ

12 Ⓐ Ⓑ Ⓒ Ⓓ

13 Ⓐ Ⓑ Ⓒ Ⓓ

14 Ⓐ Ⓑ Ⓒ Ⓓ

15 _____

_____

_____

_____

_____

_____

_____

_____

16 Ⓐ Ⓑ Ⓒ Ⓓ

17 Ⓐ Ⓑ Ⓒ Ⓓ

18 _____

_____

_____

_____

_____

_____

_____

_____

19 Ⓐ Ⓑ Ⓒ Ⓓ   **20** Ⓐ Ⓑ Ⓒ Ⓓ   **21** Ⓐ Ⓑ Ⓒ Ⓓ

22 Ⓐ Ⓑ Ⓒ Ⓓ   **23** Ⓐ Ⓑ Ⓒ Ⓓ   **24** Ⓐ Ⓑ Ⓒ Ⓓ

25 _____

_____

_____

_____

_____

_____

_____

_____

_____

26 Ⓐ Ⓑ Ⓒ Ⓓ   **27** Ⓐ Ⓑ Ⓒ Ⓓ   **28** Ⓐ Ⓑ Ⓒ Ⓓ

29 Ⓐ Ⓑ Ⓒ Ⓓ   **30** Ⓐ Ⓑ Ⓒ Ⓓ   **31** Ⓐ Ⓑ Ⓒ Ⓓ

32 Ⓐ Ⓑ Ⓒ Ⓓ

33 _____

_____

_____

_____

_____

_____

_____

_____

_____

34 Ⓐ Ⓑ Ⓒ Ⓓ   **35** Ⓐ Ⓑ Ⓒ Ⓓ   **36** Ⓐ Ⓑ Ⓒ Ⓓ

37 Ⓐ Ⓑ Ⓒ Ⓓ   **38** Ⓐ Ⓑ Ⓒ Ⓓ

PRACTICE TEST 1: WRITING

1
_____

_____

_____

_____

_____

_____

_____

_____

_____

_____

_____

_____

_____

_____

_____

_____

_____

_____

_____

_____

_____

_____

2   Ⓐ   Ⓑ   Ⓒ   Ⓓ   **3**   Ⓐ   Ⓑ   Ⓒ   Ⓓ   **4**   Ⓐ   Ⓑ   Ⓒ   Ⓓ

5   Ⓐ   Ⓑ   Ⓒ   Ⓓ

6

_____

_____

_____

_____

_____

_____

_____

_____

_____

_____

_____

_____

_____

_____

_____

_____

_____

_____

_____

_____

_____

7 Ⓐ Ⓑ Ⓒ Ⓓ   **8** Ⓐ Ⓑ Ⓒ Ⓓ   **9** Ⓐ Ⓑ Ⓒ Ⓓ

10 Ⓐ Ⓑ Ⓒ Ⓓ   **11** Ⓐ Ⓑ Ⓒ Ⓓ   **12** Ⓐ Ⓑ Ⓒ Ⓓ

13 _____

_____

_____

_____

_____

_____

_____

_____

_____

_____

_____

_____

_____

_____

_____

_____

_____

_____

_____

_____

_____

_____

PRACTICE TEST 2: READING

1 Ⓐ Ⓑ Ⓒ Ⓓ   **2** Ⓐ Ⓑ Ⓒ Ⓓ   **3** Ⓐ Ⓑ Ⓒ Ⓓ

4 Ⓐ Ⓑ Ⓒ Ⓓ

5 _____

_____

_____

_____

_____

_____

_____

_____

6 Ⓐ Ⓑ Ⓒ Ⓓ   **7** Ⓐ Ⓑ Ⓒ Ⓓ

8 _____

_____

_____

_____

_____

_____

_____

_____

9 Ⓐ Ⓑ Ⓒ Ⓓ   **10** Ⓐ Ⓑ Ⓒ Ⓓ   **11** Ⓐ Ⓑ Ⓒ Ⓓ

12 Ⓐ Ⓑ Ⓒ Ⓓ

13 _____
_____
_____
_____
_____
_____
_____
_____
_____

14 Ⓐ Ⓑ Ⓒ Ⓓ   **15** Ⓐ Ⓑ Ⓒ Ⓓ   **16** Ⓐ Ⓑ Ⓒ Ⓓ

17 Ⓐ Ⓑ Ⓒ Ⓓ

18 _____
_____
_____
_____
_____
_____
_____
_____

19 Ⓐ Ⓑ Ⓒ Ⓓ **20** Ⓐ Ⓑ Ⓒ Ⓓ **21** Ⓐ Ⓑ Ⓒ Ⓓ

22 Ⓐ Ⓑ Ⓒ Ⓓ **23** Ⓐ Ⓑ Ⓒ Ⓓ **24** Ⓐ Ⓑ Ⓒ Ⓓ

25 Ⓐ Ⓑ Ⓒ Ⓓ **26** Ⓐ Ⓑ Ⓒ Ⓓ

27 _____

_____

_____

_____

_____

_____

_____

_____

_____

28 Ⓐ Ⓑ Ⓒ Ⓓ **29** Ⓐ Ⓑ Ⓒ Ⓓ **30** Ⓐ Ⓑ Ⓒ Ⓓ

31 Ⓐ Ⓑ Ⓒ Ⓓ **32** Ⓐ Ⓑ Ⓒ Ⓓ

33 _____

_____

_____

_____

_____

_____

_____

PRACTICE TEST 2: WRITING

1

_____

_____

_____

_____

_____

_____

_____

_____

_____

_____

_____

_____

_____

_____

_____

_____

_____

_____

_____

_____

_____

_____

_____

_____

2 Ⓐ Ⓑ Ⓒ Ⓓ

3 Ⓐ Ⓑ Ⓒ Ⓓ

4 Ⓐ Ⓑ Ⓒ Ⓓ

5 Ⓐ Ⓑ Ⓒ Ⓓ

6

_____

_____

_____

_____

_____

_____

_____

_____

_____

_____

_____

_____

_____

_____

_____

_____

_____

_____

_____

_____

_____

_____

_____

_____

7 Ⓐ Ⓑ Ⓒ Ⓓ   **8** Ⓐ Ⓑ Ⓒ Ⓓ   **9** Ⓐ Ⓑ Ⓒ Ⓓ

10 Ⓐ Ⓑ Ⓒ Ⓓ   **11** Ⓐ Ⓑ Ⓒ Ⓓ   **12** Ⓐ Ⓑ Ⓒ Ⓓ

13 _____

_____

_____

_____

_____

_____

_____

_____

_____

_____

_____

_____

_____

_____

_____

_____

_____

_____

_____

_____

_____

_____

_____

_____

ANSWER KEY
PRACTICE TEST 1: READING

Question No.	Type	Content Standard	Content Standard Benchmark(s)	Key
1	Extended Response	Reading Applications: Informational, Technical and Persuasive Text	D	E
2	Multiple Choice	Acquisition of Vocabulary	A	C
3	Multiple Choice	Acquisition of Vocabulary	A	B
4	Multiple Choice	Reading Process	A	A
5	Multiple Choice	Reading Applications: Informational, Technical and Persuasive Text	B	B
6	Multiple Choice	Reading Applications: Informational, Technical and Persuasive Text	D	D
7	Multiple Choice	Reading Process	B	C
8	Multiple Choice	Reading Applications: Informational, Technical and Persuasive Text	A	B
9	Multiple Choice	Acquisition of Vocabulary	C	D
10	Short Answer	Reading Process	A	S
11	Multiple Choice	Reading Applications: Literary Text	C	C
12	Multiple Choice	Reading Applications: Literary Text	A	A
13	Multiple Choice	Reading Process	A	C
14	Multiple Choice	Acquisition of Vocabulary	A	B

Question No.	Type	Content Standard	Content Standard Benchmark(s)	Key
15	Extended Response	Reading Applications: Literary Text	A	E
16	Multiple Choice	Reading Applications: Literary Text	F	A
17	Multiple Choice	Reading Process	B	C
18	Short Answer	Reading Applications: Literary Text	C	S
19	Multiple Choice	Acquisition of Vocabulary	A	B
20	Multiple Choice	Reading Applications: Literary Text	A	D
21	Multiple Choice	Reading Applications: Literary Text	A	B
22	Multiple Choice	Reading Process	A	B
23	Multiple Choice	Acquisition of Vocabulary	E	C
24	Multiple Choice	Reading Applications: Literary Text	A	B
25	Short Answer	Reading Process	A	S
26	Multiple Choice	Reading Applications: Literary Text	F	B
27	Multiple Choice	Reading Applications: Literary Text	A	A
28	Multiple Choice	Reading Applications: Informational, Technical and Persuasive Text	D	D
29	Multiple Choice	Reading Process	B	B
30	Multiple Choice	Acquisition of Vocabulary	A	C
31	Multiple Choice	Reading Applications: Informational, Technical and Persuasive Text	A	A

Question No.	Type	Content Standard	Content Standard Benchmark(s)	Key
32	Multiple Choice	Reading Applications: Informational, Technical and Persuasive Text	D	C
33	Short Answer	Reading Applications: Informational, Technical and Persuasive Text	D	S
34	Multiple Choice	Acquisition of Vocabulary	A	C
35	Multiple Choice	Reading Applications: Literary Text	A	A
36	Multiple Choice	Reading Process	A	D
37	Multiple Choice	Acquisition of Vocabulary	C	A
38	Multiple Choice	Reading Applications: Literary Text	F	A

ANSWER KEY
PRACTICE TEST 1: WRITING

Question No.	Type	Content Standard	Content Standard Benchmark(s)	Key
1	Writing Prompt	Writing Applications / Writing Conventions	E	P
2	MC	Writing Processes	B	B
3	MC	Writing Processes	E	C
4	MC	Writing Processes	E	D
5	MC	Writing Processes	D	C
6	Short Answer	Writing Processes	A	S
7	MC	Writing Processes	C	C

Question No.	Type	Content Standard	Content Standard Benchmark(s)	Key
8	MC	Writing Processes	E	D
9	MC	Writing Processes	C	B
10	MC	Writing Processes	C	A
11	MC	Writing Processes	A	B
12	MC	Writing Processes	C	A
13	Writing Prompt	Writing Applications / Writing Conventions	C	P

ANSWER KEY
PRACTICE TEST 2: READING

Question No.	Type	Content Standard	Content Standard Benchmark(s)	Key
1	Multiple Choice	Reading Applications: Literary Text	A	A
2	Multiple Choice	Reading Process	A	C
3	Multiple Choice	Reading Applications: Literary Text	B	C
4	Multiple Choice	Reading Process	B	D
5	Short Answer	Reading Applications: Literary Text	F	S
6	Multiple Choice	Acquisition of Vocabulary	A	B
7	Multiple Choice	Reading Applications: Literary Text	C	B
8	Extended Response	Reading Applications: Literary Text	C	E

Question No.	Type	Content Standard	Content Standard Benchmark(s)	Key
9	Multiple Choice	Acquisition of Vocabulary	A	C
10	Multiple Choice	Reading Applications: Literary Text	A	A
11	Multiple Choice	Reading Applications: Informational, Technical and Persuasive Text	D	B
12	Multiple Choice	Reading Process	A	A
13	Short Answer	Acquisition of Vocabulary	D	S
14	Multiple Choice	Reading Process	B	D
15	Multiple Choice	Reading Informational, Technical Application and Persuasive Text	D	C
16	Multiple Choice	Acquisition of Vocabulary	A	C
17	Multiple Choice	Reading Applications: Informational, Technical and Persuasive Text	D	A
18	Extended-Response	Reading Applications: Informational, Technical and Persuasive Text	D	E
19	Multiple Choice	Reading Applications: Informational, Technical and Persuasive Text	B	A
20	Multiple Choice	Reading Applications: Literary Text	B	A
21	Multiple Choice	Reading Process	A	C
22	Multiple Choice	Acquisition of Vocabulary	A	D
23	Multiple Choice	Reading Process	A	A
24	Multiple Choice	Acquisition of Vocabulary	C	C
25	Multiple Choice	Reading Applications: Literary Text	F	B

Question No.	Type	Content Standard	Content Standard Benchmark(s)	Key
26	Multiple Choice	Reading Applications: Literary Text	C	A
27	Short Answer	Reading Process	B	S
28	Multiple Choice	Reading Process	B	D
29	Multiple Choice	Reading Applications: Informational, Technical and Persuasive Text	A	B
30	Multiple Choice	Reading Applications: Informational, Technical and Persuasive Text	B	A
31	Multiple Choice	Reading Applications: Informational, Technical and Persuasive Text	B	C
32	Multiple Choice	Acquisition of Vocabulary	A	C
33	Short Answer	Reading Process	A	E
34	Multiple Choice	Reading Process	A	B
35	Multiple Choice	Acquisition of Vocabulary	A	A
36	Multiple Choice	Reading Process	B	B
37	Multiple Choice	Reading Applications: Informational, Technical and Persuasive Text	A	A
38	Multiple Choice	Reading Applications: Informational, Technical and Persuasive Text	B	D

ANSWER KEY
PRACTICE TEST 2: WRITING

Question No.	Type	Content Standard	Content Standard Benchmark(s)	Key
1	Writing Prompt	Writing Applications / Writing Conventions		P
2	MC	Writing Processes	B	D
3	MC	Writing Processes	E	A
4	MC	Writing Processes	E	D
5	MC	Writing Processes	D	C
6	Short Answer	Writing Processes	A	S
7	MC	Writing Processes	C	D
8	MC	Writing Processes	D	C
9	MC	Writing Processes	D	A
10	MC	Writing Processes	C	B
11	MC	Writing Processes	C	D
12	MC	Writing Processes	C	A
13	Writing Prompt	Writing Applications / Writing Conventions		P

Index

Photo Credits

"The Six Nations of the Iroquois" (p. 12) by the New York Public Library.

"Curious Crop Circles (p. 16) by ©iStockphoto.com/George Cairns.

"Excerpt from 'The False Gems'" (p. 33) by ©iStockphoto.com/Rasmus Rasmussen.

"The Coolest Invention" (p. 46) courtesy Carrier Corporation.

"The Thinking Spot" (p. 49) by ©iStockphoto.com/Jan Ball.

"Unwinding Our Minds" (p. 73) by ©iStockphoto.com/Jamie Wilson.

"Tarantula Tamer" (p. 75) by ©iStockphoto.com/David Haynes.

"Daydreams Save the Day" (p. 111) by ©iStockphoto.com/Amanda Rohde.

"All About the Music" (p. 152) by ©iStockphoto.com/Galina Barskaya.

"Superstition Mission" (p. 197) by ©iStockphoto.com/Jaimie D. Travis.